AF601619

DENTICLE & DIE EDGE IMPRESSIONS
MORGAN DOLLAR ATTRIBUTION GUIDE

1921 P VAM 3ER Denticle Impressions IT
Denticle Field Lines

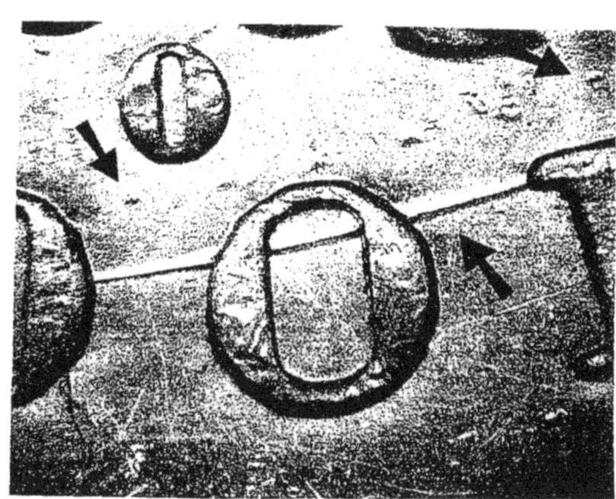

1881 O VAM 18A Denticle & Die Edge Impressions

By

Leroy Van Allen

September 2009

Updated & Expanded
September 2015

1878 S VAM 17B Denticle Impressions Neck

1878 S VAM 17B Denticle Impressions OLL

1890 O VAM 1C Double Row Denticle Impressions

1889 O VAM 9C Triangular Denticle Impressions

Published by

Rare Coin Investments (RCI)
P.O. Box C
Ironia, NJ 07845

Copyright © 2025 by Michael S. Fey, Ph.D.

Authors: Leroy C. Van Allen
Edited by: Michael S. Fey, Ph.D.

All rights reserved. No part of this book may be reproduced, by and any means, without written permission, except by a reviewer who wishes to quote brief excerpts in connection with a review or newspaper and acknowledges this publication as a source.

ISBN-13 number: 979-8-9919648-7-6

Printed in the United States

TABLE OF CONTENTS

DENTICLE AND DIE EDGE IMPRESSIONS MORGAN DOLLAR ATTRIBUTION GUIDE

INTRODUCTION

The denticle space and die edge impressions found on some of the reverse dies of the Morgan dollar are treated in this Guide. Denticle space impressions are **raised dots**, usually in the shape of a triangle, wedge, crescent, circle or flat rectangle that occur in the **coin fields in a line**. They have with the **same spacing** of 0.030" between the dots as the denticles near the coin edge. Die edge impressions are a **raised slightly curved line** below the line of denticle impressions or sometimes as an isolated line. They were caused by the accidental light impact of the obverse die denticles and/or die edge that lightly impressed the various dot shapes or lines in the reverse die during the installation of the obverse die in the coining press.

This is another major revision to this document. There are added 19 more denticle space impression die varieties for a total of 66. Also added are one more die denticle impression with die edge impression and four ***possible*** denticle impression with die edge impression nearby. Most denticle impressions are now listed as sub-varieties because they tend to disappear with die wear, except for a couple cases of deep and bold impressions.

New chapters have been added that explain in detail the causes and characteristics of denticle space and die edge impressions. Diagrams, photographs of actual Morgan dollar dies, measurements of denticle space and die edge details on coins taken thru a stereo microscope and close-up photographs of denticle spaces and rim edges of coins are provided in these new chapters: **What Are Denticle Impressions?, Anatomy of Morgan Dollar Die, Die Basining And Polishing Effects** and **How Denticle Space Impressions Happened.**

The denticle impressions were first reported by John Roberts in December 2001 on the reverse of an 1878 S VAM 17 die variety. **VAM** denotes a dollar die variety taken from the initials of the last names of the authors and as listed and described in the so-called VAM book, *Comprehensive Catalog & Encyclopedia of Morgan & Peace Dollars* by Leroy C. Van Allen & A. George Mallis, DLRC Press, third edition, 1992, and WorldWide Ventures reprint third edition, 1998, plus the yearly VAM Varieties Supplements beginning in 1999 by Leroy Van Allen. Roberts had pointed out a series of bars in several rows around OLL in DOLLAR that were later measured to match the denticle spacing.

This 1878 S VAM 17 has, by far, the most denticle space impressions raised dots, bars and lines on the reverse and is the only Morgan dollar variety with confirmed denticle space impressions on the obverse. There have been 65 more denticle impressions varieties reported beginning in 2004 for the dates from 1878 thru 1921. There are likely more denticle impressions varieties waiting to be discovered.

Webster's Dictionary defines denticle as "a conical pointed projection". On the Morgan dollar coin, the denticles appear as a row of short raised bars with rounded ends perpendicular to the coin edge and going completely around the coin adjacent to the raised rim. There are narrow spaces between each denticle. On the working dies, the **denticles** are **depressed** cavity bars next to the **depressed rim** ring with the **spaces** between these denticle cavities that are **above them** and on the same level as the die fields. It is these denticle spaces that contact another die and cause the indents in the die field which show on a coin as raised dots of various shapes in a line. For convenience, these raised dots on a coin are referred to as **denticle impressions** as an abbreviated designation of raised dots in a line with 0.030" spacing caused by the basined and polished die spaces above and between the denticle cavities.

There are a number of **axioms** that have guided the examination and analysis of Morgan dollar dies and coins in the preparation of this denticle space and die edge impressions Guide:

- The die is the die is the die– as stated by John Roberts
  - Unique polishing lines, gouges, breaks, cracks and doubled features can positively identify a specific basined and polished die used in coining presses.
  - Unfortunately actual Morgan dollar used dies and photographs of used dies are rarely available for study.
- A struck coin is an accurate **three-dimensional mirror image** of the die face of a basined and polished die.
  - Coins accurately reflect the design detail, identifying marks and wear state of the working dies.
- A single die or coin design details often may not be sufficient information to prepare accurate general conclusions.
  - Extrapolation of a single die or single coin features may not apply to many dies or coins and can lead to false general conclusions.
  - Examination of numerous coins is usually required to establish general features or trends and to check validity of conclusions.

All of the 47 denticle impression die varieties listed in the previous January 2013 edition of this Guide were refuted, except the 1881 O VAM 18A, in the document, *Off-Center and Multi Denominational Clashed Dies,* by Kevin Flynn, published by Kyle Vick, 2013. The basis for refuting the denticle impressions was an examination of a single pair of obverse and reverse 1883 CC Morgan dollar dies with flat roughly rectangular denticle spaces, but denticle spaces on coins were not examined. Either these dies had not been basined and polished or were severely over polished as evidenced by spaces between the tail feathers. Lack of examination of numerous coins to determine the usual basined and polished denticle spaces of various shapes led to erroneous conclusions that the denticle spaces were flat and rectangular which seldom is the case. Thus, the refuting of the listed die denticle impressions has an in-correct basis and is entirely erroneous.

None of the denticle impression die varieties are included in the two books, *The Top 100 Morgan Dollar Varieties: the VAM Keys* by Michael Fey and Jeff Oxman, 1996, plus the 2000 book, *SSDC Official Guide to the Hot 50 Morgan Dollar Varieties* by Jeff Oxman since denticle impressions were first reported after these books were published. The 1878 S VAM 17 is included in the book, *Official Guide To The Morgan Dollar Hit List 40* by Jeff Oxman, 2009.

Major objectives of this Guide are to make collectors aware of this interesting die variety type, explain in detail how denticle impressions and die edge impressions occurred, to point out what to look for on the coins and to serve as a reference catalogue. Recognition is given to those collectors who reported the 66 denticle impressions and five die edge impressions varieties. The various types of denticle impressions is reviewed and the **King of Denticle Impressions**, the **1878 S VAM 17**, is described in detail. The causes of denticle and die edge impressions is explored in detail in several new chapters along with ways to measure raised dots spacing on coins to ensure they match the spacing of the denticles. A section of the collection of denticle impression photographs for all reported denticle impression varieties is included to allow quick attribution of coins. Descriptive listings of all the known denticle impressions varieties is followed by the last two sections of detailed photographs of each variety in chronological order.

The author can be contacted about possible new denticle/die edge impressions die varieties at:
Leroy Van Allen, P.O. Box 196, Sidney, OH 45365 or by e-mail at vams@woh.rr.com

REPORTING OF DENTICLE IMPRESSIONS DIE VARIETIES

The very **first** denticle impressions on a Morgan dollar was reported in December 2001. John Roberts sent an 1878 S on December 12, 2001 for examination that he thought was a VAM 17 but had *"several characteristics not mentioned in the book".* He stated that there were *"a number of odd 'lumps' on both sides.... with marks around the date and inside the lower loops of both 8's... under the tail feathers... around and inside the O in DOLLAR."* His first thought was *"that these were re-polished clash marks, but they don't appear to have the correct orientation with the opposing die."* But he went on to say *"I'm stumped."*

My reply letter to John Roberts on December 16, 2001 assigned a new sub-variety designation of VAM 17A to the coin with a description of *"Slightly raised denticle impressions thru OLL in DOLLAR, below OL and four slanted impressions below left tail feathers."* My comments were: *"hadn't noticed slightly raised small areas around OLL and below left tail feathers before.... Don't think they are clash marks....They seem to match the shape and spacing of denticles... I think the die was accidently hit several times with the edge of a hub to create these raised marks.... I see couple of raised lines in 8-8, but don't think they are worth photographing and mentioning in description.... A whole new category of variety!"*

So this 1878 S VAM 17 was the first to be reported for a **new variety category of denticle impressions** on the reverse. Unfortunately the few slight marks on the obverse were not recognized as denticle impressions at that time because the obverse die had been polished somewhat. Also, the cause of the denticle impressions from a hub turned out to be incorrect because the hub is like a coin with **raised rim** that would prevent the denticles from contacting a die field. Besides, the dies were inspected several times during and after the hubbing operations which surely would have resulted in the reverse die being discarded. It was later determined that the most likely source of denticle impact on a working die field would be from **another working die denticle spaces** which are at the same level as the die fields and **above** the **recessed** denticle bars and rim.

But that isn't the end of the 1878 S VAM 17 story! In July 2009 Jason Henrichsen pointed out that there were denticle impressions on the Liberty head neck edge with the same spacing as the denticles on an 1878 S VAM 17A he sent for examination. Shortly thereafter, Brian Raines, in early August 2009, sent a different die state 1878 S VAM 17A with *"denticle clashes at date, STATES, A, ONE, UNI".* As a result of these two coins, two more VAM 17 sub-varieties were added with **VAM 17B** the **earliest** denticle impressions based on Brian Raine's coin with at least **13** denticle impressions on the obverse and **43** on the reverse. Jason Henrichsen's coin resulted in **VAM 17C** listing with later **slightly polished** VAM 17B that removed most of the denticle impressions at the date and weakened ones on reverse. The **VAM 17A** was ***revised*** as the **late** die state of denticle impressions with only shallow dots inside of the lower loop of both 8's and only denticle impressions at OLL and below left tail feathers still remaining. The **1878 S VAM 17A, B, C** is the **King Of Denticle Impressions**!

The next denticle impressions variety reported was much later when Bill Fivaz on March 6, 2004 sent an 1921 P Morgan dollar he said *"It has a series of raised dots (clashmarks) leading from the left bow up to the left branch. I can't figure out whence they came!"* My reply on March 14, 2004 listed it as a new variety 1921 P VAM 40A with denticle impressions on reverse with letter stating, *"Raised triangles below left tail feathers are impressions of outside of denticle."*

Two more denticle impressions varieties were reported later in 2004, the 1878 P VAM 225A by Michael Fahey in October 2004 and the 1921 P VAM 31A by Leroy Van Allen from John Kohut's coin in November 2004. Since then, new denticle impressions varieties have been reported every year. The following list in chronological date order gives the date, variety designation, who reported and date reported for each of the known varieties (Includes some different die states for 1878 S VAM 17A, B, C and 1904 O VAMs 12 & 22A1 & 22A2 and 1921 P VAM 31A1 & 31A2 & 31B.). Although the denticle impressions likely happened when the dies were first installed in the coining presses, they have been mostly assigned sub-varieties since they usually disappeared from die wear. A couple varieties have such bold denticle impressions that lasted the die lifetime and are included in main die variety listing. A couple listings have two or more sub-variety listings because die state changes.

DENTICLE IMPRESSIONS DISCOVERERS HALL OF FAME

1878 P VAM 221A	Brian Raines	October 2007	
1878 P VAM 225A	Michael Fahey	October 2004	
1878 CC VAM 20A	Russell James	April 2010	
1878 S VAM 17A	John Roberts	December 2001	
1878 S VAM 17B	Brian Raines	August 2009	
1878 S VAM 17C	Jason Henrichsen	July 2009	
1878 S VAM 34A	Brent Fogelberg	June 2015	
1879 P VAM 57A	John Roberts	June 2007	
1881 O VAM 18A	Brian Raines	March 2012	
1883 O VAM 2A	Jason Henrichsen	November 2010	
1884 P VAM 8J	Jason Keefer	December 2014	
1886 O VAM 1C	Logan McKechnie	April 2006	Possible single denticle impression
1887 P VAM 1E	Gill Medina	February 2007	
1888 P VAM 1D	Phil Perdue	July 2009	
1888 P VAM 17A	David Druzisky	February 2010	
1889 P VAM 1C1	Peter Hohnstein	March 2013	
1889 P VAM 1E	Brian Raines	September 2014	
1889 P VAM 1F	Brent Fogelberg	June 2015	
1889 P VAM 5D	Jason Henrichsen	November 2012	
1889 P VAM 5E	Jason Keefer	August 2013	
1889 P VAM 14A	Jason Keefer	March 2013	
1889 P VAM 18B	Jason Henrichsen	February 2012	
1889 P VAM 62	Brian Raines	December 2014	
1889 O VAM 9B	John Roberts	March 2006	
1889 O VAM 9C	Leroy Van Allen	February 2013	William Ennett coin (updated Brent Fogelberg June 2015)
1889 O VAM 13F	John Vernieri	February 2009	
1889 O VAM 16A	Logan McKechnie	August 2009	
1890 P VAM 1C	Ron Fisher	April 2008	
1890 P VAM 1D	Dominick Luckette	July 2010	
1890 P VAM 1E	David Druzisky	September 2010	
1890 P VAM 1F	David Druzisky	September 2010	
1890 P VAM 1G	Peter Hohnstein	December 2010	
1890 P VAM 1I	David Close	September 2011	
1890 P VAM 4A	Ash Harrison	April 2008	
1890 P VAM 11A	Brian Raines	December 2009	
1890 O VAM 1C	David Close	January 2006	
1890 O VAM 1G	Brain Raines	April 2011	
1890 O VAM 1H	Bill Latour	March 2013	
1890 O VAM 1 I	Brian Raines	August 2015	
1890 O VAM 2B	Brian Raines	October 2013	
1890 O VAM 16B	Brian Raines	October 2013	
1890 O VAM 28B	Jason Keefer	November 2013	
1890 O VAM 33A	William Ennett	June 2012	
1891 P VAM 1B	Bill Latour	September 2008	
1891 P VAM 6A	Brian Pfendler	September 2011	
1891 P VAM 6B	Nick Capuano	March 2014	
1891 O VAM 5A	David Druzisky	July 2010	
1894 O VAM 11B	John Coxe	February 2011	
1900 O VAM 21E	Bill Latour	June 2009	
1900 O VAM 35	Bill Latour	September 2013	
1900 O VAM 47B	Bill Latour`	June 2015	

1901 O VAM 1B	David Druzisky	March 2010	
1901 O VAM 11A	David Druzisky	May 2010	
1901 O VAM 45	Bill Latour	September 2008	
1902 O VAM 44B	John Coxe	March 2010	
1902 O VAM 90A	Peter Hohnstein	October 2013	
1903 P VAM 1B	David Close	March 2010	
1904 O VAM 12	Michael Ash	May 2007	Revised for denticle impression
1904 O VAM 22A1	Mike Andrews	January 2005	
1904 O VAM 22A2	Michael Ash	May 2007	
1904 O VAM 30A	Michael Ash	May 2007	
1904 O VAM 30B	Jason Henrichsen	July 2009	
1921 P VAM 3F2	Leroy Van Allen	October 2006	George Powell coin
1921 P VAM 3CW2	Jason Henrichsen	October 2009	
1921 P VAM 3ER	John Roberts	August 2008	
1921 P VAM 3GM	Daniel Peltier	December 2014	
1921 P VAM 31A1	Leroy Van Allen	November 2004	John Kohut coin
1921 P VAM 31A2	John Coxe	January 2008	
1921 P VAM 31B	John Coxe	January 2008	
1921 P VAM 40A	Bill Fivaz	March 2004	
1921 S VAM 1AJ	Laurence Galbraith	September 2006	

REPORTING OF DIE EDGE IMPRESSIONS DIE VARIETIES

The reporting of die gouges/scratches on the Morgan dollar reverse dies has occurred for well over 50 years. It is only fairly recently that some of the reverse gouges/scratches were identified as actually **direct impressions** of the **edge of the obverse die** and not the typical grazing or glancing blow from various objects, including the obverse die edge.

In June 2007, John Roberts had identified an 1879 P of Sandra Sulak's coin that had *"unlisted series of denticle impressions to right of olive leaves"*. This coin was sent by Sandra Sulak in July 2007 for listing and photographs. There were four unlisted raised triangle dots to the right of the top leaves along with an unlisted doubled date and Phrygian cap top. It was assigned VAM 57 and the denticle impressions as 57A. In the description of 57A the author noted that, *"Diagonal die scratch to left of denticle impressions possible caused at same time as denticle impression from die edge."*. This was the **first mention** of **die edge impression** associated with denticle impressions and has the correct spacing below the denticle impressions of 0.025" as currently measured.

A very **unusual** case is the 1881 O VAM 18A with denticle impressions above a **pronounced** raised line below them. The 1881 O VAM 18 was reported by Martin Field in August 1980 with a fairly strongly doubled 18 and a long bold die gouge thru DOL in DOLLAR on the reverse as listed and pictured in the VAM book. Then in March 2012, Brian Raines sent an EDS PL of the 1881 O VAM 18 with the notation that it was *"not a die gouge on the rev. It is a rim & denticle clash."* It showed a row of six denticle impressions above the line thru DOL with the correct 0.030" denticle spacing and 0.025" distance above the die rim edge line. These weak denticle impressions wore away quickly on the die since they were near the periphery letters where the die wear is strongest. The VAM book original photograph of the line didn't show clear raised triangle denticle impressions because of die wear. This variety has the **boldest raised line** below the row of denticle impressions of any reported die variety!

A similar example of denticle impressions with associated die edge impression to the 1879 P VAM 57A is the 1890 P VAM 1D. It was originally reported in July 2010 by Dominick Luckette for denticle impressions at the olive including a faint raised dot above the row of three triangles. But in December 2012 the author noticed a faint die edge impression line at about 0.025" below the denticle impressions. It is very close to the same location as the die edge impression of the 1879 P VAM 57A.

Another example of die edge impression below denticle impressions is the 1921 S VAM 1AJ. It was originally reported by Laurence Galbraith in September 2006 for denticle impressions above the top arrow feather. The author also noticed in December 2012 that a short line at the end of the top arrow feather was the correct distance of about 0.025" below the denticle impressions and was likely caused by the obverse die edge.

A more recent reported fifth example of denticle impressions with die edge line below is the 1890 O VAM 1 I. It was reported in August 2015 by Brian Raines with new denticle impressions below the olive branch. The author also noticed a rim line below the two denticle impressions with correct 0.025" spacing.

There are also some examples of obverse die edge impressions on the reverse die close to the denticle impressions but not directly below. Four have been reported and listed so far. The 1889 O VAM 9C was initially reported by Leroy Van Allen in February 2013 as a weak denticle impression. A better example coin with clearer additional denticle impressions was reported by Brent Fogelberg in June 2015 and Van Allen also noticed a possible die edge line below the denticle impressions. In March 2013, Bill Latour reported an 1890 O VAM 1H with denticle impressions and possible die edge lines at the left edge of the eagle's left leg. Also, in March 2013 Jason Keefer reported an 1889 P VAM 14A with denticle impressions and possible die edge line at the first left leaf cluster of the left wreath. He also reported an 1889 P VAM 5E in August 2013 with denticle impressions and possible die edge lines at the left and right of the wreath bow.

Some due edge lines may be **located far** from the denticle impressions if the obverse die edge contacted the reverse die separately from the denticle impressions. But these possible cases are not conclusive as the known ones generally don't have the long curved lines of a die edge and are not listed in this document.

A more plausible case of separate die edge impression would be a fairly long raised line on the reverse die with a **slight curvature** and **higher middle and tapered ends**. These would be similar to the Peace dollar reverse die edge impressions that have been reported on the obverse die upper part. For these Morgan dollar cases, the obverse die would have to be tilted enough so that only the die edge contacted the reverse die. The curve middle of the die edge impression could be at the top or bottom depending which way the obverse die was tilted. A separate listing of 13 cases of possible die edge impressions that was selected by the author is shown in the accompanying list along with who originally reported them and when.

A section at the end of this document, **Photographs of Denticle Die Edge Impressions**, shows the five examples of die edge impressions with the denticle impressions above them, four examples of denticle impressions with possible die lines associated with them, plus the 13 selected possible die edge impressions without associated denticle impressions.

DIE EDGE IMPRESSIONS DISCOVERERS HALL OF FAME

Die varieties with die edge line below denticle impressions (reporting of denticle & line association):

1879 P VAM 57A	John Roberts	June 2007 (denticle impressions)
1879 P VAM 57A	Leroy Van Allen	July 2007 (die edge line)
1881 O VAM 18	Martin Field	August 1980 (die gouge)
1881 O VAM 18A	Brian Raines	March 2012 (denticle & die edge impressions association)
1890 P VAM 1D	Dominick Luckette	July 2010 (denticle impressions
1890 P VAM 1D revised	Leroy Van Allen	December 2012 (die edge line)
1890 O VAM 1 I	Brian Raines	August 2015 (denticle impressions)
1890 O VAM 1 I	Leroy Van Allen	August 2015 (die edge line)
1921 S VAM 1AJ	Laurence Galbraith	September 2006 (denticle impressions)
1921 S VAM 1AJ	Leroy Van Allen	December 2012 (die edge line)

Die varieties with denticle impressions and possible die edge line association nearby:

1889 P VAM 5E	Jason Keefer	August 2013
1889 P VAM 14A	Jason Keefer	March 2013
1889 O VAM 9C	Leroy Van Allen	February 2013 (initial denticle impression & later die edge line)
1889 O VAM 9C revised	Brent Fogelberg	June 2015 (more & clearer denticle impressions)
1890 O VAM 1H	Bill Latour	March 3023

Die varieties with die scratch/gouge possibly caused by die edge impressions (no denticle impressions):
(Compiled by author December 2012) Originally reported by:

1878 P VAM 7 Gouge A	Leroy Van Allen	December 1965
1879 P VAM 61 Die scratch leg	Jerry Robertson	April 2005
1884 CC VAM 4A Die gouge E	Earl Young	March 2006
1887 P VAM 26A Die gouge A	John Bradley	June 2007
1921 P VAM 1C/48 Die gouge wreath bow	Martin Field	July 1984
1921 P VAM 3H Die gouge olive leaves	Martin Field	August 1981
1921 P VAM 16 Die gouge olive branch	Terry Armstrong	June 1999
1921 D VAM 1S Die gouge ED	Jim Hart	June 2001
1921 D VAM 1AA Die gouge E	Jim Hart	June 2002
1921 D VAM 1AU Die gouge N	John Kohut	May 2004
1921 D VAM 1BD Die scratch wreath	Bill Van Note	October 2004
1921 S VAM 1CE Die scratch below O	John Baumgart	November 2011
1921 S VAM 21B Die scratch D	Bradley Graham	June 2010

WHAT ARE DENTICLE IMPRESSIONS?

There are many, many instances of small to tiny raised dots that can be seen with the naked eye or 10X loupe on Morgan dollar coins on both the obverse and reverse. These are generally of **rough tops and edges** and most frequently are associated with a **die crack** that has irregular outlines and tops. Sometimes these irregular shaped dots can be isolated and not be associated with die cracks. They are due to **isolated flaws in the die steel**, surface **imperfections as the dies wore** and rusting of the die surface that creates **rust pitting** that shows as raised irregular dots on coins. In all of these cases of tiny raised dots they have **irregular shapes and rough surfaces**. They also appear in **random locations** on **both** the obverse and reverse dies with **random patterns** of groups of raised dots.

Denticle Impressions Characteristics

But denticle impressions are a **different type** of raised dots. They are quite scarce on coins, much more so than the isolated die chips, rough dots on crack and isolated or groups of die rust pitting. Generally they have **smooth tops** and **well-defined shapes**, typically triangles. Other well defined shapes include tapered wedges, circles, crescents, and in rare cases flat short rectangles of lightly basined or over polished dies. They always appear **only in the fields** of the **reverse die**.

Another characteristic of denticle impressions is their **occurrence in a line**. Many examples show three to six raised dots all in a slightly curved line, if four or more occur together. Sometimes there will be a **second line** of weaker dots above the primary dot line with about 0.020" to 0.025" separation. This second line of weaker raised dots are most often directly above the primary line of raised dots.

A third primary characteristic of denticle impressions is a **constant separation spacing of 0.030".** Thus, the dots can not be from random die chips of die steel flaws, die wear caused dot or random die rust pitting. These raised dots therefore have to be **from a man-made object. No tool with this spacing and specific shapes is known** to have existed at the Morgan dollar die manufacturing facility at the Philadelphia Mint. One might wonder if somehow the collar that produces the coin edge reeding was the cause. But the collar that surrounds the lower die during the striking of the coins has the reeding inside the circular opening and could not contact the flat die field on the die face. The raised **dot separation distance is the same as the 0.030" separation of the denticle spaces** on coins.

Another peculiarity is where the raised dots of well defined shapes in a slightly curved line with 0.030" separation show up on the Morgan dollar dies. These occur **almost exclusively** on the lower reverse die. By far, they are **most frequently found on the lower reverse**, generally somewhat in the center of the die. A few isolated cases of smooth defined shape dots in a line occur more to the sides of the lower reverse and even up at the middle and upper reverse fields.

Still another special characteristic of the raised dots in a line is that in rare instances **a continuos raised and slightly curved line shows below the row of dots**. Typically the line is about 0.025" below the dots row whether the dots are in a horizontal line or tilted. This slightly curved line is from the outside edge of the die rim depression that creates the raised rim on coins. The curved line closely matches the radius of the die or coin rim. **No tool is known** that could create such a combination of raised dots and curved raised line. It was therefore created by the obverse die accidently contacting the reverse die field at just the correct angle to impress the rim edge and the polished denticle projections simultaneously.

It should be noted that sometimes two or more sets of denticle impression dots in a line may be found **widely separated** on the reverse of one coin. This is due to **multiple light contacts** of the obverse die by the die installer. Other rare instances show somewhat **isolated single or several** raised smooth top dots away and separated from the main line of raised dots. This could be caused by the die installer making **lightly bouncing contacts** in the fields. Sometimes contact was near the depressed devices and letters where there **would not be contact of portions** of the top obverse die with the lower reverse die as the obverse die was being installed in the coining press.

How Denticle Impressions Occurred

The dimensions, cause of various denticle space shapes and how they occurred from basining and polishing and subsequent installation in the coining presses is treated in detail with illustration and photographs in later chapters, **Anatomy of Morgan Dollar Die, Die Basining and Polishing Effects** and **How Denticle Space Impressions Happened**. Briefly, these denticle impressions were from the slightly tilted upper obverse die lightly contacting the lower reverse die fields during the installation of the obverse die in the coining presses. The basining and polishing of all Morgan working dies rounded and tapered the flat 0.010" wide and 0.025" long denticle spaces that **projected and were exposed as the tiny outermost part** of a working die. Various degrees of basining and polishing of the exposed denticle space projections **created the different shapes** on them. They show up as triangles, wedges, crescents and circles when the obverse die accidently lightly contacted the reverse die field that were raised above the depressed design and letter cavities.

Some Key Examples

A few accompanying photographs illustrate some of the denticle impression characteristics. The photograph of the **1887 P VAM 1E** clearly shows the typical denticle impression triangle shape.

The **1878 P VAM 225A** shows some wedge shaped denticles. Scarcer crescent shaped denticle impressions occurred for the **1921 P VAM 31A**. Two rows of dots of one above the other is shown for the **1890 O VAM 1C**. The lines of dots are exceptionally long with a curvature readily apparent. Sometimes only one or two raised triangles show as illustrated for the **1901 O VAM 45** with two bold triangles at the eagle's right shoulder with 0.030" spacing. Other raised triangles would have shown but the eagle's wing and neck cavities are adjacent to the two dots precluding any obverse die contact there. Another interesting case is the single raised triangle of **1904 O VAM 12** below the eagle's right wing. A slight raised area 0.030" to the left at the wing feather edge is some confirmation of a denticle impression where the right side is the eagle's leg cavity precluding any denticle impression.

Simultaneous denticle and die edge impression strongest example is the **1881 O VAM 18A.** The EDS example shows six raised dots above the strong raised line below with obvious curvature. Another good example of die edge line and denticle dot row is the **1879 P VAM 57A**. There is even evidence of a second dot row with a single dot showing above the strong row of dots closest to the raised curved line.

Further examples of denticle and die edge impressions are shown in the chapters on **Types of Denticle Impressions** and **Die Edge Impressions**. The several chapters on descriptive listings and photographs include all the reported denticle impressions die varieties to date.

1887 P VAM 1E Triangular Denticle Impressions

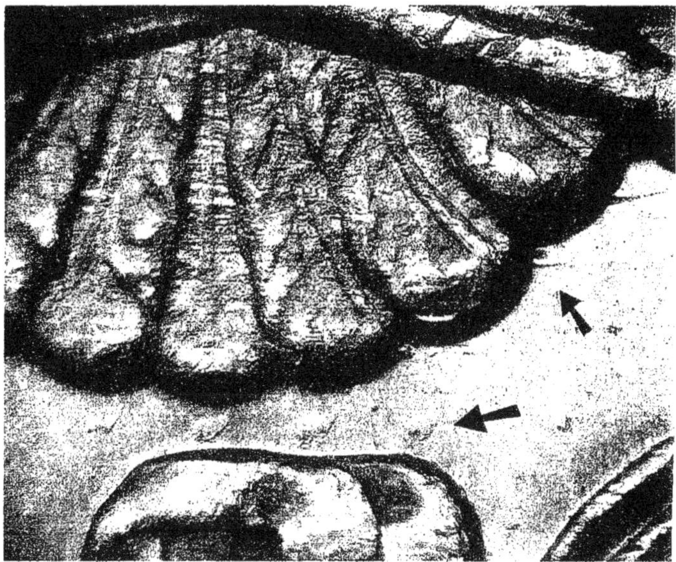

1878 P VAM 225A Wedge Denticle Impressions

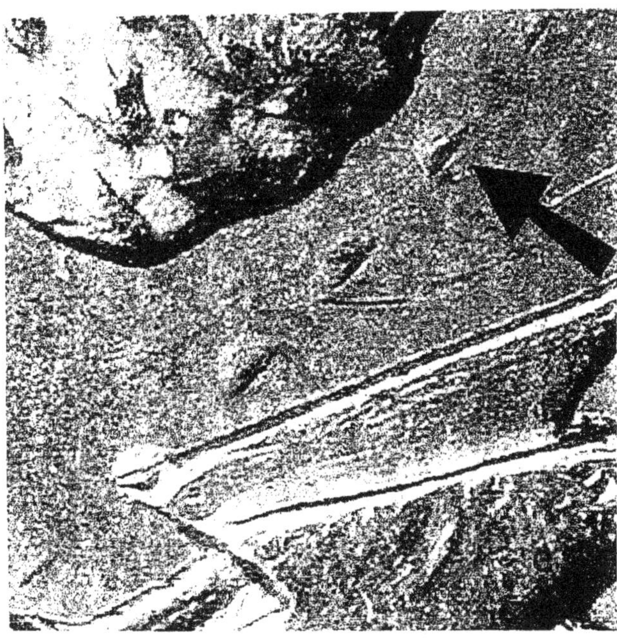

1921 P VAM 31A Crescent Denticle Impressions

1890 O VAM 1C Triangular & Dots Denticle Impressions

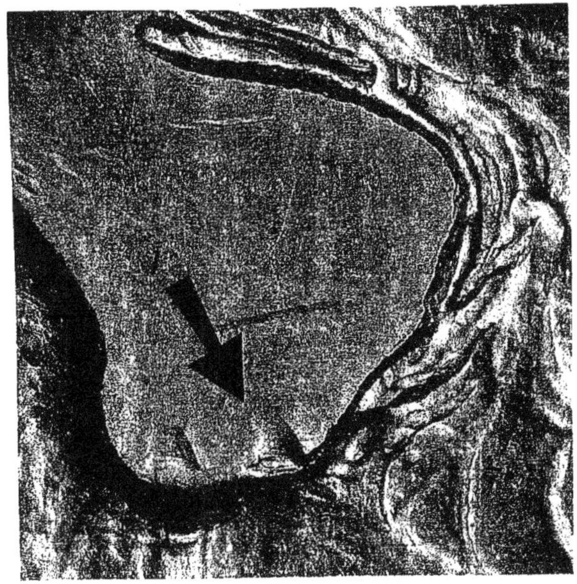

1901 O VAM 45 2 Triangular Denticle Impressions

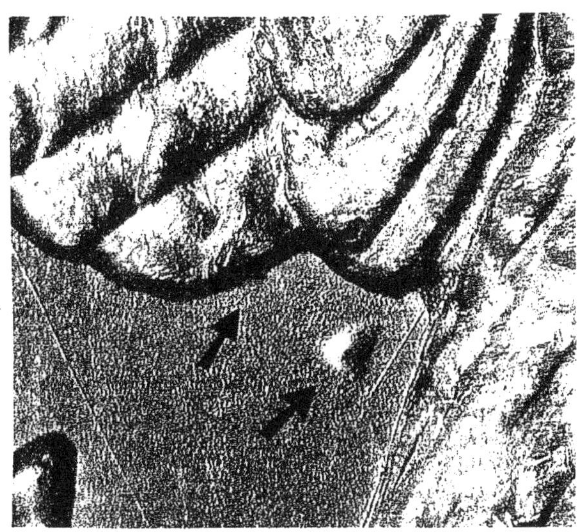

1904 O VAM 12 Triangular Denticle Impression, EDS

1881 O VAM 18A Triangular Denticle
& Die Edge Impressions

1879 P VAM 57A Triangular & Dot Denticles
& Die Edge Impressions

TYPES OF DENTICLE IMPRESSIONS

There are over 60 denticle impressions die varieties reported to date. There is only one reported so far with denticle and die edge impressions on the obverse die, the 1878 S VAM 17A, B, C. All the other denticle impressions are in a line or two on the reverse die, primarily on the lower reverse.

Location of Denticle Impressions

The most frequently reported location of a line of denticle impressions on the reverse die is **below the eagle's tail feathers**. An example is shown for the 1878 P VAM 225A. Likely it was the way the lower reverse die was oriented in the coining press with the reverse die oriented up-side-down from the coining press front. The obverse die would then be oriented with the top away from the coining press operator for a correct viewing orientation of the struck coins. As the die installer put the obverse die into the coining press, a slight tilt of the die top forward away from the installer would allow light contact of the obverse die top with the lower part of the lower reverse die that was in an up-side-down orientation. This is explained in greater detail and illustrated in the chapter, **How Denticle Space Impressions Happened.**

There are only small open die field spaces in the lower center of the reverse die below the eagle's tail feathers, wreath bow and around the olive leaf clusters and arrow heads. Although there is more open space in the larger fields at the left and right in the coin center and top, very few denticle impressions show there. An example is the 1878 S VAM 17B with possible light contact of denticles and rim edge at the reverse top left. Other examples are the 1901 O VAM 45 and 1921 P VAM 31B.

Other locations of denticle impressions include **below the eagle's right wing** for the 1879 P VAM 57A and at the **arrow heads** including 1904 O VAM 30A and 1921 P VAM 31A1. A few show denticle impressions **below the wreath bow** in the legend letters with examples for the 1904 O VAM 30B and 1878 S VAM 17A, B, C treated separately. There are even two examples with strong denticle impressions in the **middle legend letters** for 1921 P VAM 3F1 and 1921 P VAM 3ER that also shows the **field edge line of denticle cavities between the denticle space impressions** at IT. (Also 1878 CC VAM 20A at TA.) Other locations are at the **arrow feathers** with an example shown for 1890 O VAM 1G and at the **olive branches** with an example shown for 1890 P VAM 1D. **Two sets** of denticle impressions are on the 1890 O VAM 33A with one set of five raised triangles at the end of the arrow feathers and second set of five denticle impressions below the olive leaves. There are a few examples of vertical lines of denticle impressions with the rest mostly horizontal. Perhaps one of the most amazing large number of sets of denticle impressions is the 1878 S VAM 34A with six different sets of 3 to 4 denticle dots impressions spaced 0.030" on the middle and lower left reverse.

Denticle Impressions by Mint

To date, there have been reported 33 denticle impressions for the Philadelphia Mint, 29 for the New Orleans Mint, only three for the San Francisco Mint and one for the Carson City Mint plus none for the Denver Mint in 1921.

From 1878 thru 1904, the Philadelphia Mint struck almost 50% more coins than the New Orleans Mint and two and a half times the San Francisco Mint. But the dies produced for the Philadelphia and New Orleans Mints were about the same with the San Francisco Mint about 20% less. For the 1921 Morgan dollar, the coinage was about the same for the San Francisco and Denver Mints and twice as much for the Philadelphia Mint. So the denticle impressions accidents occurred at about similar rates for the Philadelphia and New Orleans Mints but much less for the San Francisco Mint which must have had more careful die installers or the coining presses of a different design that were easier to install the dies. The Philadelphia Mint has a high number of eight denticle impressions dies listed for the 1890 with a mintage of 17 million, eight denticle impressions dies listed for the 1889 with a mintage of 22 million and six denticle impression dies for the 1921 run of 40 million Morgan dollars.

1878 P VAM 225A Denticle Impressions

1878 S VAM 17B Denticle Impressions AT

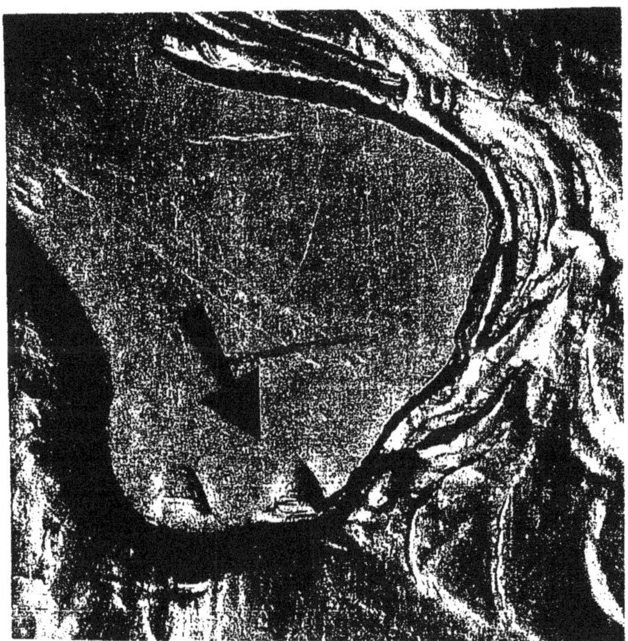

1901 O VAM 45 Two Denticle Impressions

1921 P VAM 31B Two Denticle Impressions

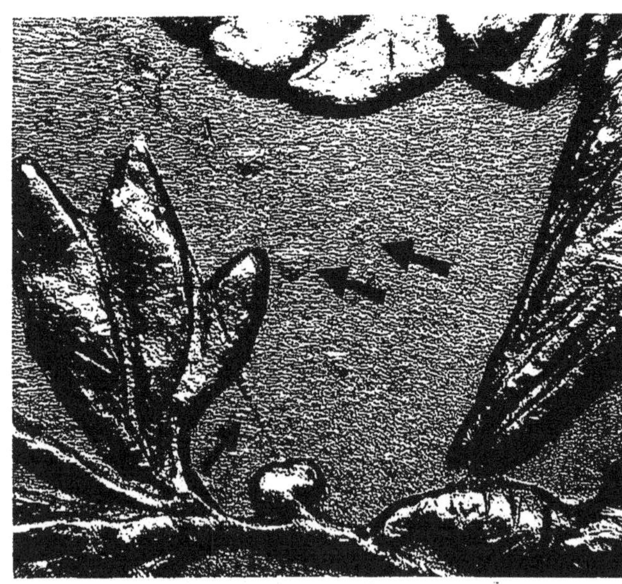

1879 P VAM 57A Denticle & Die Edge Impressions

1904 O VAM 30A Denticle Impressions

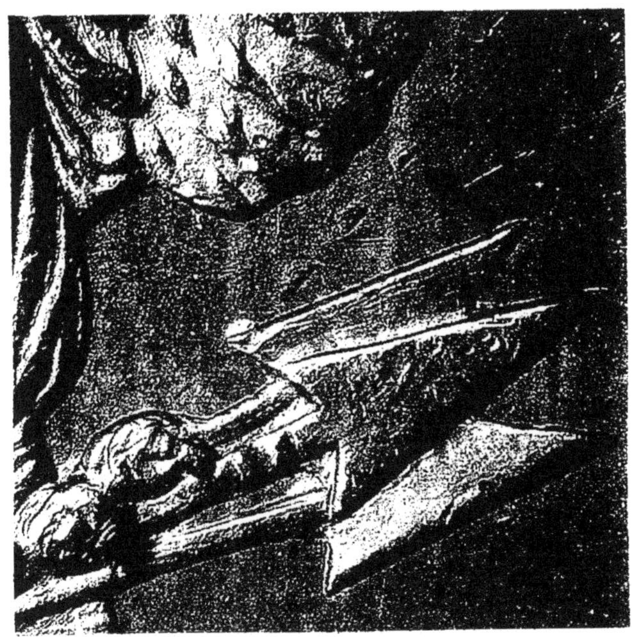
1921 P VAM 31A1 Denticle Impressions

1904 O VAM 30B Denticle Impressions E-D

1921 P VAM 3F2 Denticle Impressions ME

1921 P VAM 3ER Denticle Impressions IT

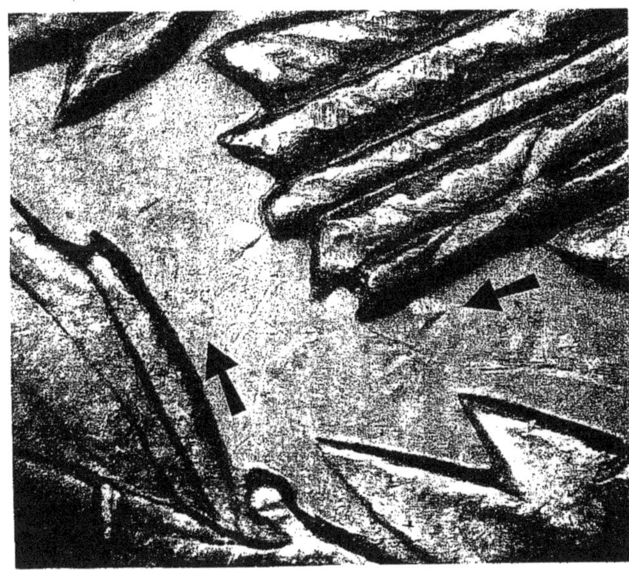
1890 O VAM 1G Denticle Impressions Arrow Feathers

1890 P VAM 1D Denticle & Die Edge Impressions

1878 S VAM 34A Three Denticle Impressions Rim– N of UNITED

1878 S VAM 34A Three Denticle Impressions Olive Leaf Cluster

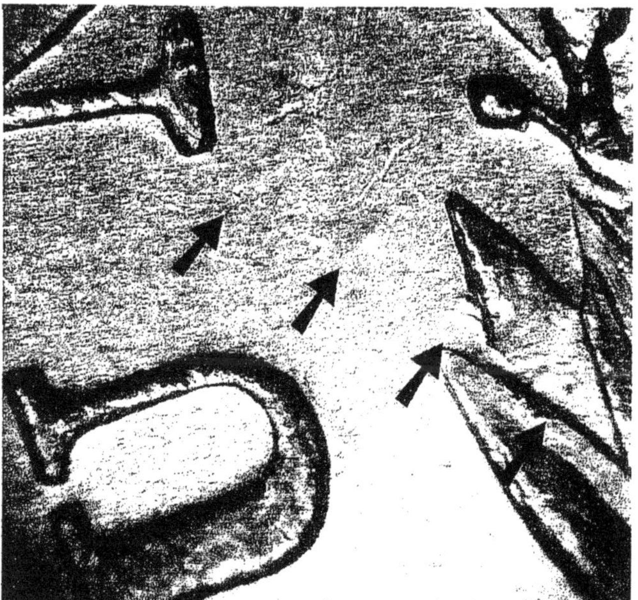
1878 S VAM 34A Four Denticle Impressions N– Wreath Leaf

1878 S VAM 34A Three Denticle Impressions Wreath– Middle Olive Leaf Cluster

1878 S VAM 34A Three Denticle Impressions U in United

1878 S VAM 34A Three Denticle Impressions E of ONE

Number of Raised Dots for a Denticle Impression

There are four die varieties with only a **single** denticle impression, with examples of 1886 O VAM 1C which is a questionable one, and the 1904 O VAMs 12 & 22A which share the same reverse die. They are listed because they have clear typical triangle shape with smooth tops of denticle impressions and not rough tops or edges of die chips. There are twelve cases of only **two** raised dots denticle impressions space 0.030" apart, such as the very strong impressions at the eagle's upper right wing of 1901 O VAM 45 as previously shown, the added two impressions at the top of the eagle's right wing of 1921 P VAM 31B as previously shown and the two above the arrow feathers of 1921 S VAM 1AJ. Most of the other examples of denticle impressions have **3-7 raised dots** in a line with 0.030" separation, with the 1878 S VAM 17A, B, C being a notable exception with so many impressions.

Shapes of Denticle Impressions

The most frequent shape of a denticle impression is a **raised triangle** with an example shown for the 1889 O VAM 9C. However, some can be somewhat round in shape for the 1879 P VAM 57A or crescent rounded ends as shown for the 1921 P VAM 31A1 as previously shown. The causes of their various shapes is discussed in the chapter, **Die Basining and Polishing Effects**. Some of the impressions for the 1878 S VAM 17A, B, C are quite wide with somewhat flat ends likely due to a heavily over polished die that widened and flattened the denticle spaces.

The shape of the denticle impressions varied somewhat with the angle of the die impact and die wear, but primarily on the extent of the die basining and polishing. The **spacing between the raised dots in a line** that matches the denticle spacing of **0.030"** and generally smooth tops are the **most important factor** for variety attribution of denticle impressions. Some examples show a double line of raised dot denticle impressions with a spacing between the dot lines about the same as the denticle spacing. This was likely from the denticle spaces that contacted the reverse die field having a **slope** from die basining and polishing that allowed the inner and outer portions of the denticle space to contact the die field at the same time. Another possibility is that several contacts were made of the die field. However, usually the point of the raised triangle dots were **opposing each other**, the dots were one above the other and the spacing between the lines of dots didn't vary that much. The previous photograph shows two lines of opposing triangle dots example for the 1904 O VAM 30A.

King of Denticle Impressions, 1878 S VAM 17A, B, C

No doubt about it, the **1878 S VAM 17A, B, C** deserves the title of **King Of Denticle Impressions** simply because of the sheer **number** of raised dots and lines impressions of **56**. However, some of these likely are **die rim edge lines** or denticle spaces **impacting sideways** because of the upper obverse die inadvertently being shifted sideways from a glancing moving contact.. Plus as an added bonus, it was the **first** denticle impressions reported in December 2001 by John Roberts and so far, is the only variety with denticle impressions confirmed for the **obverse die** as reported by Jason Henrichsen in July 2009. Additional denticle impressions were reported by Brian Raines in August 2009 on both the reverse and obverse dies from his **rare early die state** of the denticle impressions. The 13 obverse and over 43 reverse denticle impressions for the earliest die state, VAM 17B, is way more than any other denticle impressions die variety! The VAM 17C has somewhat fewer impressions on the obverse from die polishing and the VAM 17A has the least impressions from further die polishing and wear.

Photographs of VAM 17B show 18 bold denticle impressions around OLL in DOLLAR and four below the tail feathers. They are fairly flat and wide rectangles from the obverse denticle spaces that had been of a severely polished die. Some rectangles are overlapping from multiple contacts of the obverse die close together as well as various locations on the reverse die. But the spacing between impressions is the correct 0.030".

There are five vertical lines with denticle spacing above ST, seven raised crescents above A and

1890 O VAM 33 Denticle Impressions Below Olive Leaves

1890 O VAM 33 Denticle Impressions Arrow Feathers

1886 O VAM 1C Raised Triangular Dot

1904 O VAM 22A Denticle Impression

1921 S VAM 1AJ Denticle Impressions Arrow Feathers

1889 O VAM 9C Four Triangular Denticle Impressions Arrow Feathers

one above the right T in STATES. Four lines show between UN and four above N in UNITED for a total of at least 43 on the reverse die. The lines at ST and N likely were from the die denticle space outside end making multiple die edge impressions at a high tilted angle in order to contact the reverse die face nearest the coining press front.

The obverse shows five impressions at the Liberty head neck edge with 0.030" spacing as shown in a photograph plus six raised dots in a band across the lower part of the date and two raised arcs at the bottom of the 7 as shown in a separate photograph. Likely some of the lines at the date middle could be from the die rim edge impressions. A possibility for the lines and dots at the Liberty head neck and date to accidently occur would be if the lower reverse die was in the stake block without a surrounding collar. This would leave the reverse die face totally exposed for it's denticle spaces and rim edges to contact the upper obverse die.

That is a total of **13 denticle space and rim edges impressions on the obverse** and at least **43 on the reverse**. It makes a **grand total 56** on this one denticle impressions variety. What an **incredible** series of denticle space and rim edge impressions for this one variety, the 1878 S VAM 17A, B, C!

1878 S VAM 17B Denticle Impressions OLL

1878 S VAM 17B Denticle Impressions TF

1878 S VAM 17B Denticle Lines Above ST

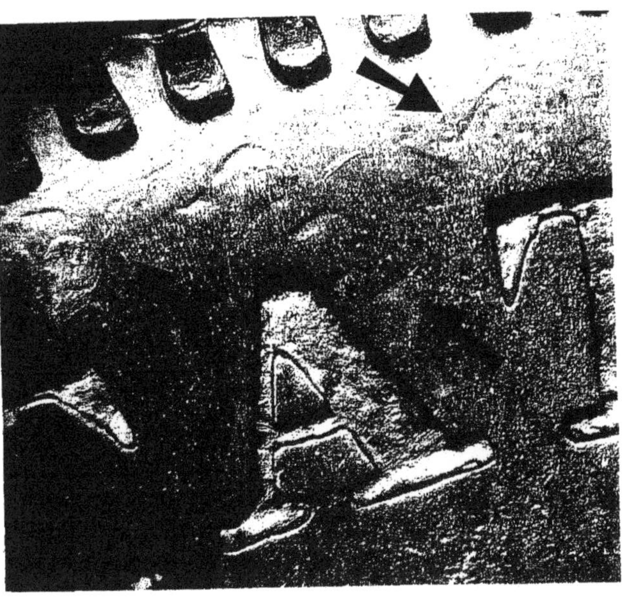

1878 S VAM 17B Denticle Impressions AT

1878 S VAM 17B Denticle Impressions UN

1878 S VAM 17B Denticle Impressions Neck

1878 S VAM 17B Denticle Impressions Date

TYPES OF DIE EDGE IMPRESSIONS

As illustrated in the chapter, **How Denticle Space Impressions Happened**, if the obverse die tilt was from 12° to 22° from the vertical, there would be possible simultaneous contact of the denticle space edges along with a rim die edge spaced about 0.025" to 0.040" below the raised dots. An obverse die tilt greater than 22° from the vertical would have always produced only the isolated rim die edge line. Between 12 ° to 22° die tilt an obverse die contact would have produced just the rim die edge line depending on the degree of denticle space deformation from die basining and polishing. Tilts of 22° or less could also have produced just the denticle space impression depending on the degree of denticle space basining and polishing.

Location of Die Edge Impressions

The **most convincing** of the die edge impressions are those **located just below a single or double row of denticle impressions**. The **first identified** curved die edge impression line in July 2007 was for the 1879 P VAM 57A located below the eagle's right wing and running thru the top olive branch leaves below the eagle's right wing. It has the correct 0.025" spacing below the denticle impression. A recently identified as a die edge impression is the gouge at DOL of DOLLAR of the 1881 O VAM 18. It was first reported as a gouge in August 1980, but later identified by Brian Raines as a die edge impression in March 2012 when he saw six denticle impressions above this line on an **EDS** die as VAM 18A. It is the **boldest die edge impression reported so far** and has the correct 0.025" spacing below the row of denticle impressions. **Weak denticle impressions can disappear from die wear** as it did on later die states of the 1881 O VAM 18.

A similar example to the 1879 P VAM 57A is the 1890 P VAM 1D at about the same location at the olive leaves with a fine curved line 0.025" below the denticle impressions. The 1921 S VAM 1AJ has a short line at the end of the upper arrow feather with a spacing of 0.025" below the two denticle impressions above the upper arrow feather. A recently reported 1890 O VAM 1 I has two denticle impressions at about the same location and a die edge line to the left.

An 1889 P VAM 5E has a possible die edge scratch to the left of the denticle impressions at the wreath bow, an 1889 P VAM 14A denticle impression at the first left wreath leaf cluster with a possible die edge line above, an 1889 O VAM 9C has four strong triangle denticle impressions at the arrow feather ends with a possible curved die edge line below and an 1890 O VAM 1H with denticle impressions above the top olive leaf cluster and three possible die edge lines at eagle's right leg left edge. These four possible die edge lines with denticle impressions have photographs in the last chapter, **Photographs of Denticle and Die Edge Impressions.**

Other possible die edge impressions are **fine lines widely separated** from the denticle impression. These could be due to separate contacts with the obverse die edge causing raised lines on the coins. Some of these include the 1878 P VAM 225A with fine lines at the tail feathers above the denticle impressions, 1878 S VAM 17B with a few fine lines at the edges of the date digits, above ST in STATES and at UN of UNITED, 1890 P VAM 1F with two horizontal lines above the denticle impressions, 1890 P VAM 11A with faint line below denticles at left top of wreath bow, 1890 O VAM 33 with gouges on the eagle and the 1904 O VAM 30B with die scratches at the top wing edge. These and additional ones are all shown in the section on **Photographs of Denticle Impressions Die Varieties.**

Die Edge Only

There is also the possibility that the obverse die edge was struck and impressed into the reverse die **without including any denticle impressions**. This would be possible if the obverse die happened to be **tilted enough upon contact** with the reverse die to only impress the die edge. This is illustrated in the chapter, **How Denticle Space Impressions Happened**. Since the obverse die edge has

1879 P VAM 57A Denticle & Die Edge Impressions

1881 O VAM 18A Denticle & Die Edge Impressions

1890 P VAM 1D Denticle & Die Edge Impressions

1921 S VAM 1AJ Denticle & Die Edge Impressions

1890 O VAM 1 I Two Denticles & Die Edge Impressions

1889 P VAM 5E Possible Denticle & Die Edge Impressions

1889 P VAM 5E Two Denticle Impressions Bow

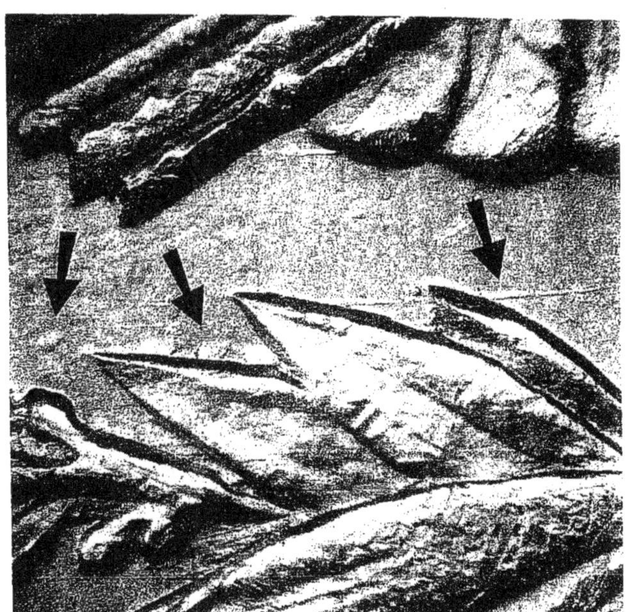

1889 P VAM 14A Possible Denticle & Die Edge Impressions

1889 P VAM 14A Denticle Impressions Below TF

1890 O VAM 1H Possible Denticle & Die Edge Impressions

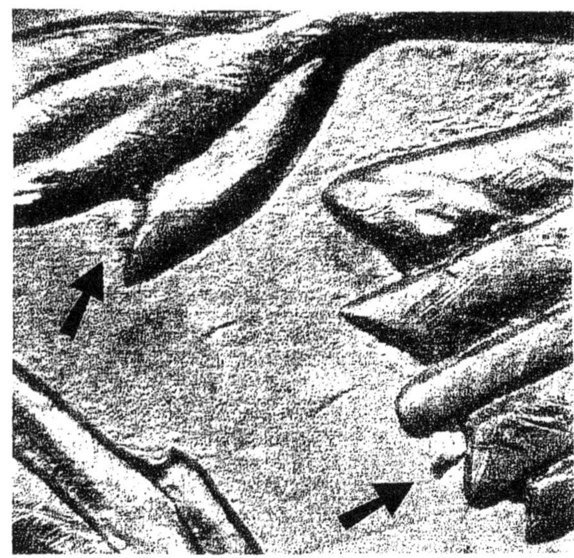

1889 O Four Triangular Denticle Impressions

1889 O VAM 9C Possible Curved Die Edge Impression

1889 O VAM 9C Possible Die Edge Scratches Eagle's Leg

1889 O VAM 9C Triangular Inner & Outer Obverse Denticle Spaces

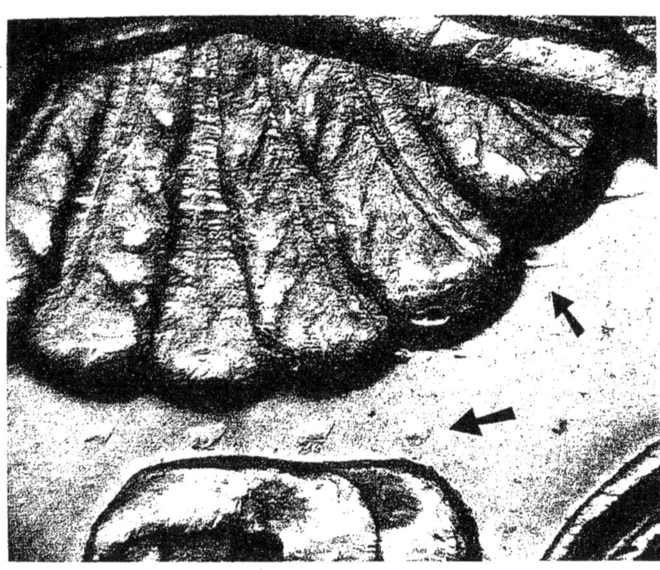

1878 P VAM 225A Denticle Impressions, Possible Die Edge Lines

1878 S VAM 17B Denticle Impressions, Possible Die Edge Lines

1878 S VAM 17B Possible Denticle Edge Lines Above ST

1878 S VAM 17B Possible Die Edge Lines UN

1890 P VAM 11A Denticle Impressions, Possible Die Edge Line

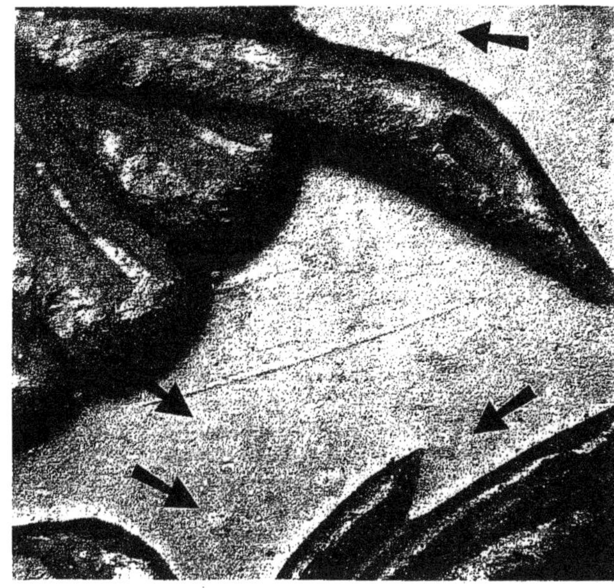

1890 P VAM 1F Denticle Impressions, Possible Die Edge Lines

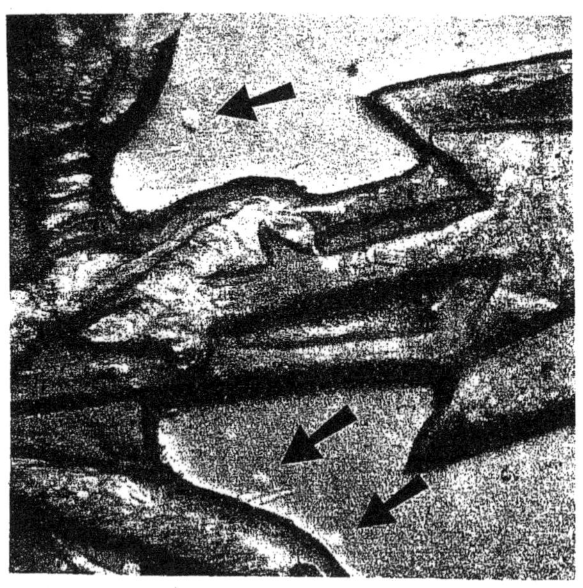

1890 P VAM 1F Denticle Impressions at Leg

1890 O VAM 33 Denticle Impressions at Olive Leaves Ends

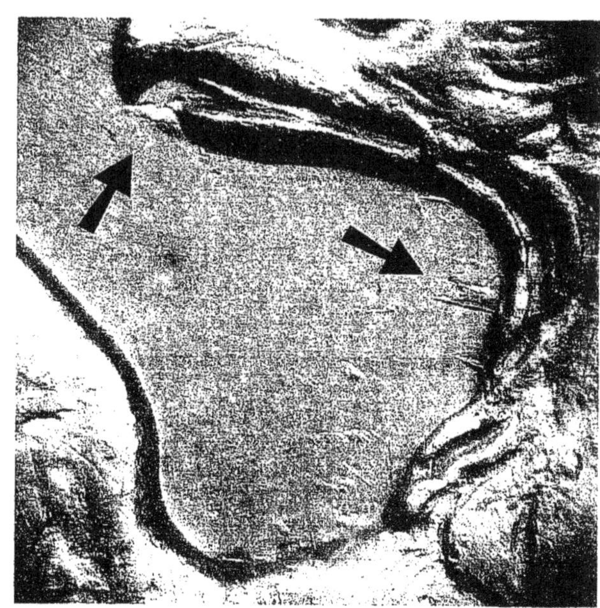
1890 O VAM 33 Possible Die Edge Lines Eagle's Neck

1890 O VAM 33 Denticle Impressions Arrow Feathers

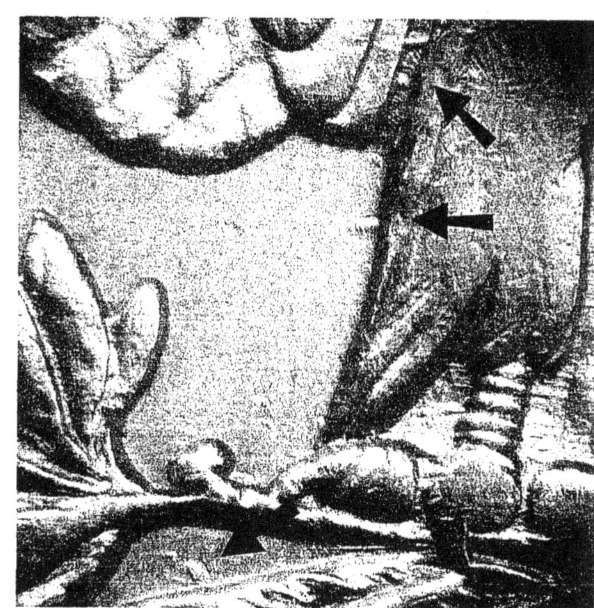
1890 O VAM 33 Possible Die Edge Lines Below Wing

1904 O VAM 30B Possible Die Edge Lines Wing Edge

1904 O VAM 30B Denticle Impressions E-D

curvature, the die edge impression would be slightly curved with higher raised center of the impression on coins with shallower tapered ends. This is clearly shown for the 1881 O VAM 18B/43. Also the die edge curve middle could be at the top or bottom of the impression depending upon the tilt of the obverse die upon impacting the reverse die.

There is also the possibility that the obverse die edge could have had a glancing or grazing impact on the reverse die causing a straight line die scratches or gouges. However, it would be very difficult to differentiate this grazing scratch from scratches by other objects, including polishing grits. So these straight line gouges and scratches are not listed or pictured as separate die edge impressions or gouges.

A section at the end of this document, **Photographs of Denticle and Die Edge Impressions,13 Possible Edge Only** shows 13 possible examples selected by the author of only die edge curved line impressions without denticle impressions and not any glancing or grazing straight gouges or scratches. An example of a possible obverse die edge impressions is for the 1921 D VAM 1AA with a curved line at E of ONE.

Most of the isolated single die edge impressions are at the lower reverse. But three are at the top of the reverse with reversed curvature, 1878 P VAM 7, 1884 CC VAM 4A and 1921 S VAM 1CE. Two curved lines are at TED of UNITED for 1921 D VAM 1S.

Die Edge Impressions by Mint

There are five positive identified die denticle spaces with die edge impressions, four denticle impressions with possible die edge impressions and 13 selected possible die edge impressions alone. Those with denticle impressions with a die edge impression include two for the Philadelphia Mint, two for the New Orleans Mint and one for the San Francisco Mint. The possible denticle impressions with die edge impression have two for Philadelphia Mint and two for the New Orleans Mint. Those selected for possible die edge only include six for the Philadelphia Mint, four for the Denver Mint, two for the San Francisco Mint and one for the Carson City Mint.

1921 D VAM 1AA Possible Curved Die Edge Line

ANATOMY OF MORGAN DOLLAR DIE

In order to determine what caused these raised dots of various shapes in a slightly curved line on the coin reverses, the details of the Morgan dollar working die face that has been basined and polished needs to be examined. **Alternatively**, numerous **Morgan dollar coins** can be examined as they would show the **working die face** design details and die state **in 3D mirror images**. The author does not own a Morgan dollar die or currently have access to one for examination. However, the author did have access to a canceled 1878 CC reverse die 1 in the mid-1970s owned by a collector. Photographs of this Morgan die were taken of the side and top die face as shown in the accompanying illustrations. This allows some of the **major working die dimensions** to be obtained by measuring the 2X actual size of the die top and side view features.

The Morgan dollar coin diameter is a nominal 1.5 ". With the die photographs of 3" die face diameter, measurements taken off the photograph only need to be divided by 2 for actual die dimensions.

Another close-up photograph of a Morgan dollar die is in the book, *Mint Mark "CC"*, by Howard Hickson, 1972, Nevada State Museum. On page 44 is a slightly larger than 2X oblique photograph of an 1884 Morgan dollar obverse die marked No 38. This photograph was useful in checking die rim and denticle lengths when copied and re-printed at 2X actual size.

Measurement Tools

Since the U.S. (English) system of measurement was in use at the Philadelphia Mint at the early time period of 1878- 1904 Morgan die production, all dimensions are in this measurement system of inches and not the metric system of centimeters. A conventional ruler in inches is sufficient to measure the overall die dimensions from available die photographs.

To measure the die rim, denticles and denticle spaces on die photographs and coins requires use of more accurate measurement tools than conventional rulers. Rim and denticle dimensions need to be measured with an **accuracy of about one-thousandths of an inch**. The author used a Brown & Sharpe caliper with scale divisions of 0.001 inch and a mini-scale tool for microscopes with divisions of 0.005 inches. These measurement tools are shown in the accompanying photographs.

The mini-scale accuracy was checked with the caliper as shown in a photograph with the caliper set to 0.030" against the mini-scale markings above. It shows the mini-scale markings were accurate to about 0.001". The interpolation between the mini-scale markings at 0.010" and 0.005" intervals can be accurate to about 0.002" to 0.003".

Die Overall Dimensions

An accompanying diagram shows the overall dimensions of a Morgan dollar cylindrical working die profile as scaled off the 1878 CC die 2X photograph. The overall die length was 2" with a base diameter of 1.75". The die face diameter was 1.50", the same as the Morgan dollar coin diameter. This die face diameter continued as a cylinder for 0.25" height to a tapered shoulder of about 0.31" height to the main body of the die. It is likely these overall working die dimensions are applicable for the Morgan dies made from 1878- 1904.

Attempts were made to measure the die edge rim widths and height plus the denticle lengths from these photographs. But as shown in the close-up photographs, the mini-scale measurements on the 2X photographs were **just an approximation** because of the lack of close-up detail of the photographs.

The clearest close-up photograph was of the rim and denticle lengths of the 1884 obverse die that may not have been basined and polished. It showed a rim and denticle length of both of 0.025" after division by 2 for the 2X photograph.

An enlarged print of the 1878 CC die photograph die shows **over polished denticles** at the

Canceled 1884 Morgan Dollar Obverse Die

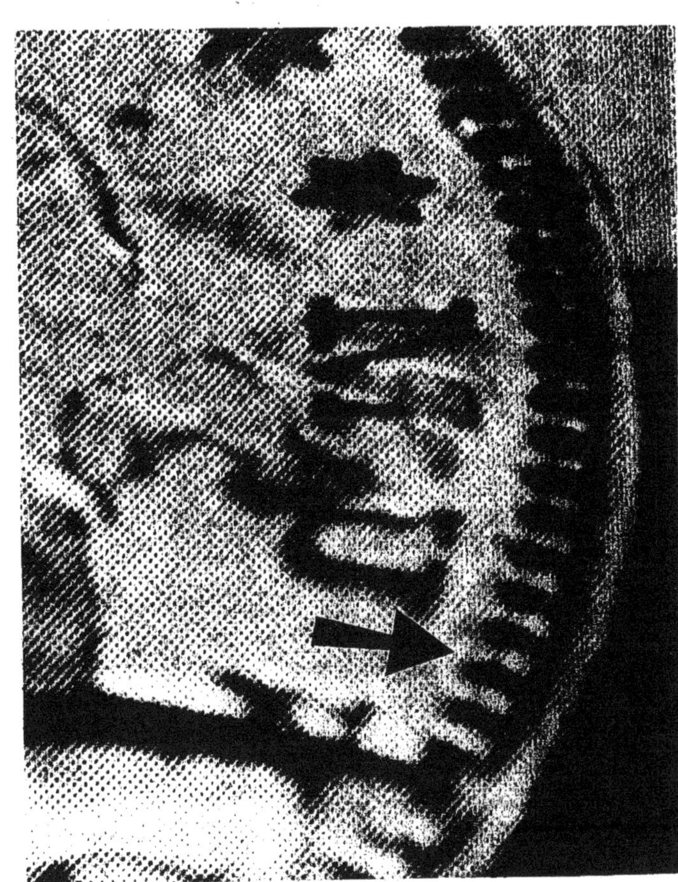

1884 Morgan Dollar Obverse Die Denticle Spaces

Canceled 1878 CC Die Face

Canceled 1878 CC Die 1

Brown & Sharpe Caliper 0.001" Scale Divisions

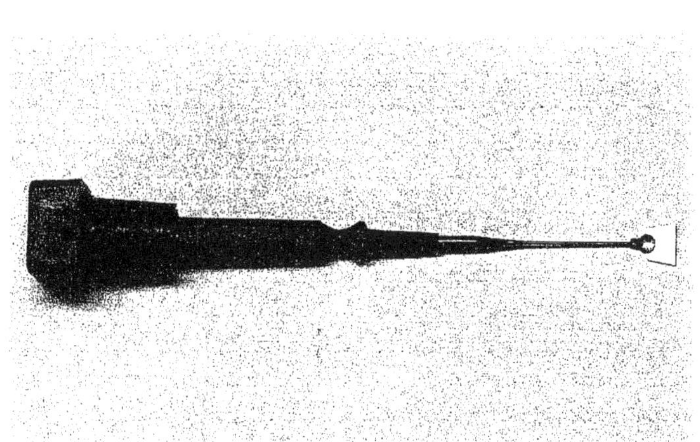

Mini-Scale Tool For Microscopes

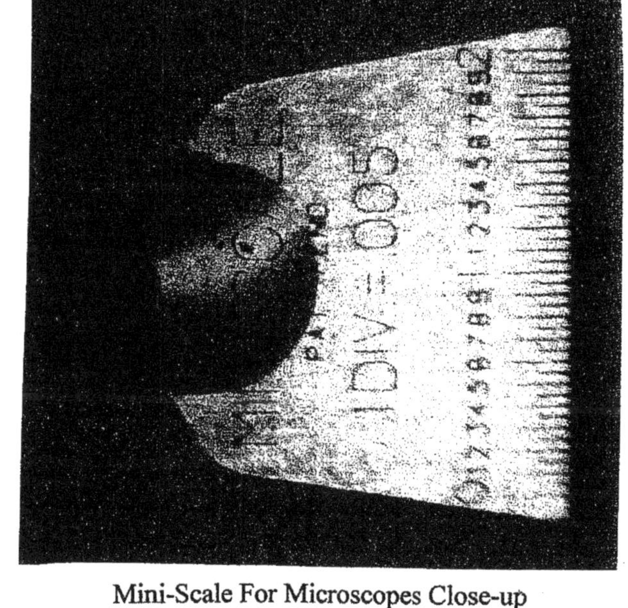

Mini-Scale For Microscopes Close-up

Caliper Reading 0.030"

Mini-Scale Compared to Caliper 0.030"

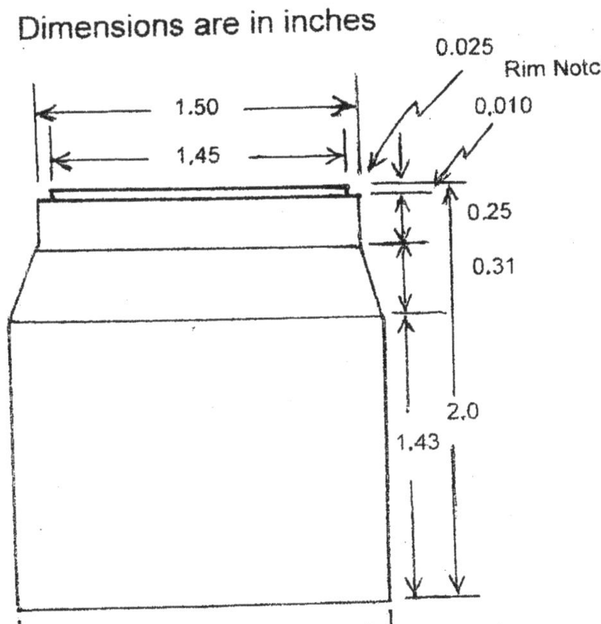

Morgan Dollar Die Overall Dimensions

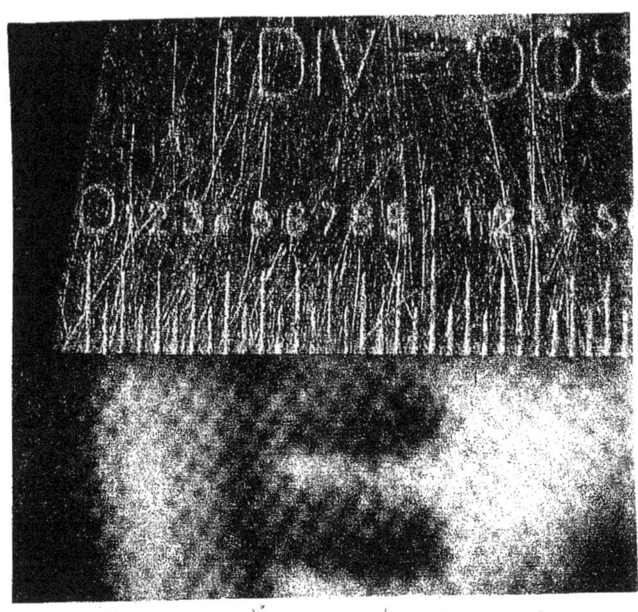

1884 Morgan Obverse Die 2X Photograph
Rim Edge & Denticle Lengths 0.050" & 0.050"

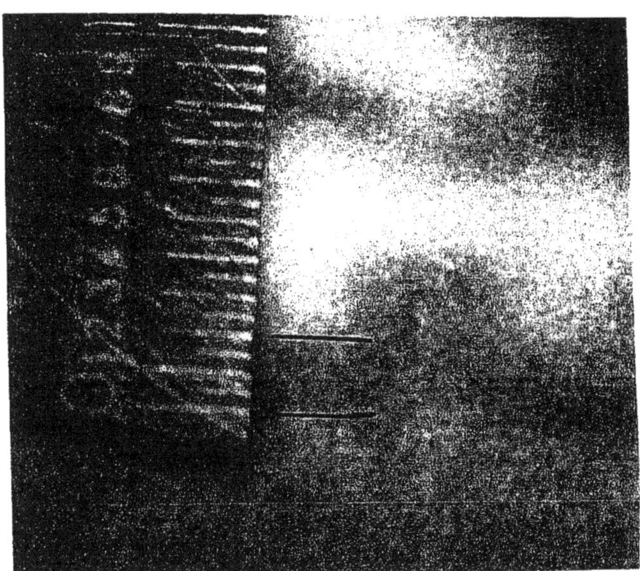

1878 CC Morgan Reverse Die 2X Photograph
Rim Edge Height 0.020"

1878 CC Morgan Reverse Die 2X
Rim Edge & Denticle Lengths 0.050" & 0.050"

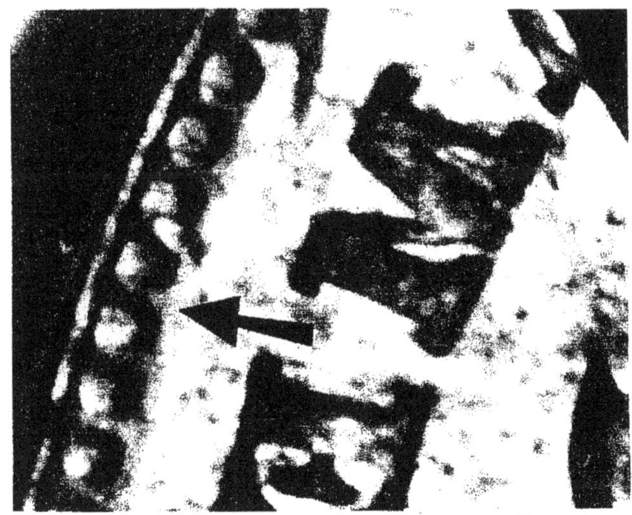

1878 CC Morgan Reverse Die, Full Denticles
Triangular & Wedge Shaped Denticle Spaces

1878 CC Morgan Reverse Die, Over Polished Denticles

eagle's right wing tip and **full denticles** at the other side near AME of AMERICA. These full denticles showed some **partially closed-up denticle spaces** and not the full open flat denticle spaces at the other side of the die at the eagle's right wing tip. It is likely this working die was basined and polished. The enlarged photograph of the 1884 obverse showed mostly flat and open denticle spaces, possibly of an un-basined and un-polished die..

Rim, Denticles and Denticle Space Measurements

Accurate measurements of the die rim, denticles and denticle spaces was made using full struck rim and denticle coins. These coins reflect the **actual dimensions** of the Morgan working die when full formed and **basined and polished** for use in the coining presses.

A series of photographs show the mini-scale dimensions when **superimposed on the coins** with digital photographs taken thru a 10X stereo microscope. Coins of 1879 P, 1902 O and 1921 P that had **full struck rim and denticles** with **mostly open denticle spaces** were selected for measurement. Accuracy of the measurements were 0.001" at the 0.01" and 0.005" markings with interpolations between markings of about 0.002" to 0.003". Measurements were rounded off to nearest 0.005" for a three coin average of dimensions. But most measurements were at the 0.005" and 0.01" dimensions that were likely the standard size for Morgan working dies. The resulting average measurements were:

Rim width 0.025"
Denticle length 0.025"
Denticle width 0.020"
Denticle space width 0.010"
Distance between denticle spaces 0.030"

There remained to be measured the **rim and denticle heights**. Denticle spaces are at the die field level, **if flat and not beveled from the die basining and polishing**. These heights were a challenge to measure with the two measurement tools available. The mini-scale couldn't be used to measure vertical distances on the coin inside, because of the flat scale metal dimensions extending outside and beyond the accurate markings.

Instead, the caliper was used in conjunction with spacers of accurate thickness coated paper of 0.020" with double stick tape on one side. The tape allowed the spacers to be secured at various places on the coins without damaging the surfaces.

Coins were selected for measurement that had **full rims and denticles on opposite sides** of the obverse and reverse. The small 0.020" thick spacers were placed in the field close to the denticles. They had to be on the field between the letters or stars on the coin and thus were fairly narrow. The thickness of the rim was measured directly with the caliper. Measurement between the obverse and reverse spacers at the adjacent fields next to the denticles were made with the caliper with an accuracy of about 0.001" to 0.002". Morgan dollar coin dates measured were 1880 P, 1881 P, 1889 P, 1889 S, 1902 O and 1921 P to obtain the rim height.

The rim height above the field was calculated by subtracting the two spacers total distance of 0.040" from the thickness of the field adjacent to the denticles and then subtracting this from the total rim thickness and dividing by 2 to obtain the **average single rim thickness** of the obverse and reverse. The **measured rim height** for these **six basined coins was 0.010" to 0.011"**.

Another set of coins with full rims and denticles on opposite sides were measured for **rim and denticle height** above the adjacent coin field. This was to obtain the denticle thickness, rim thickness and the notch distance of the denticles below the rim top. Coins measured were 1878 S, 1883 P, 1890 P and 1902 O. The rim thickness was measured and calculated as before. The denticle thickness was calculated by subtracting the two spacers thickness of 0.040" from the total coin thickness at the denticle tops, and then subtracting the two spacers thickness of 0.040" from the total coin thickness at the adjacent field, and finally subtracting this field measurement from the denticle measurement and dividing by two to obtain the **average single denticle thickness** of the obverse and reverse.

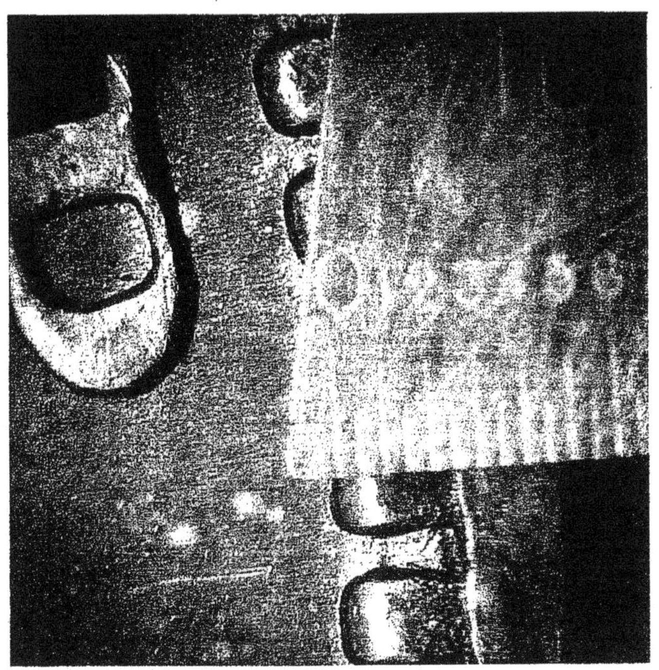

1879 P Denticle Length 0.025"

1879 P Rim Width 0.025"

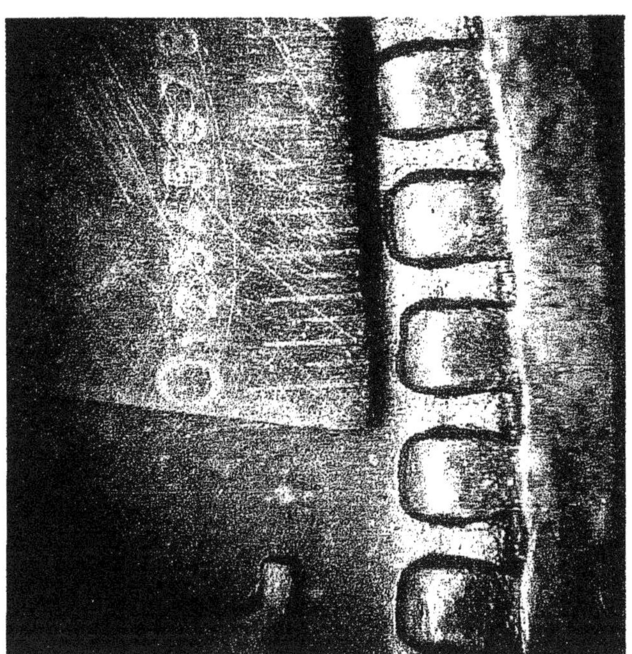

1879 P Denticle Width 0.020"

1879 P Distance Between Denticle Spaces 0.030"

1879 P Denticle Space Width 0.010"

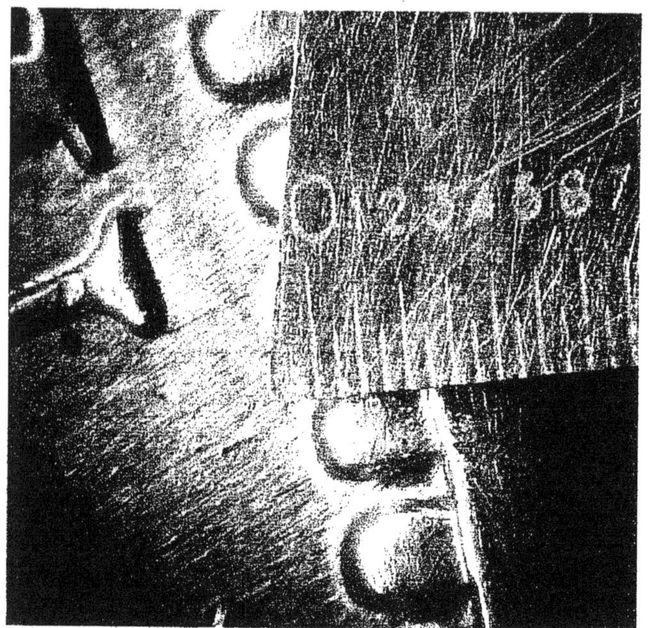

1902 O Denticle Length 0.025"

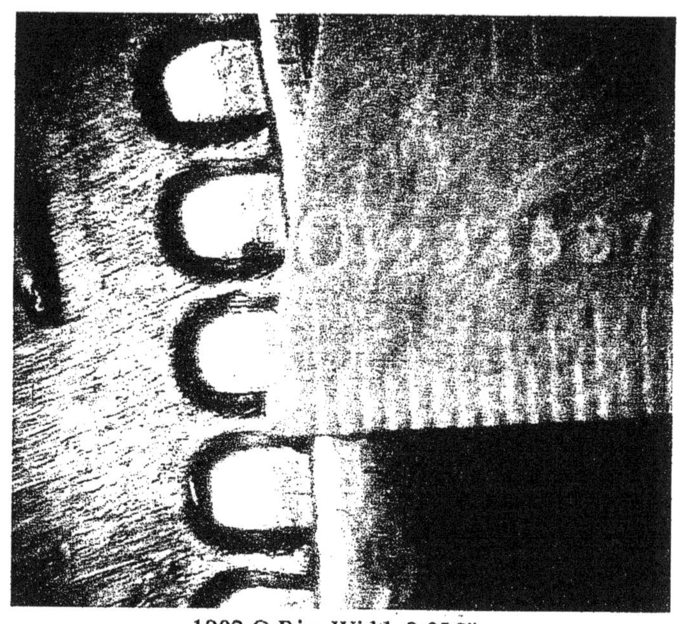

1902 O Rim Width 0.025"

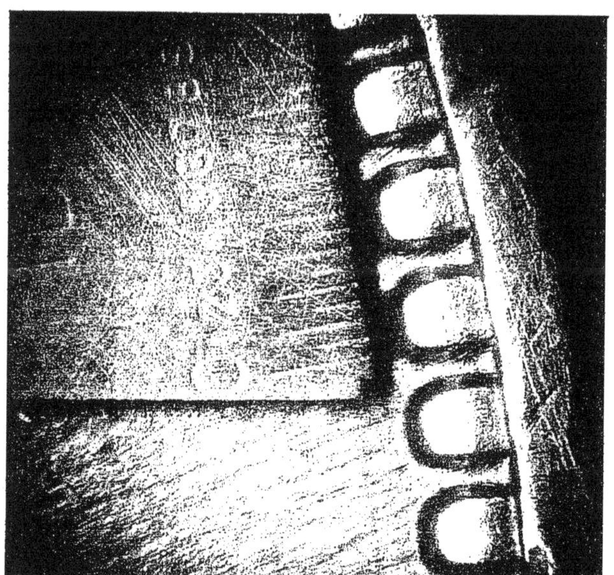

1902 O Denticle Width 0.020"

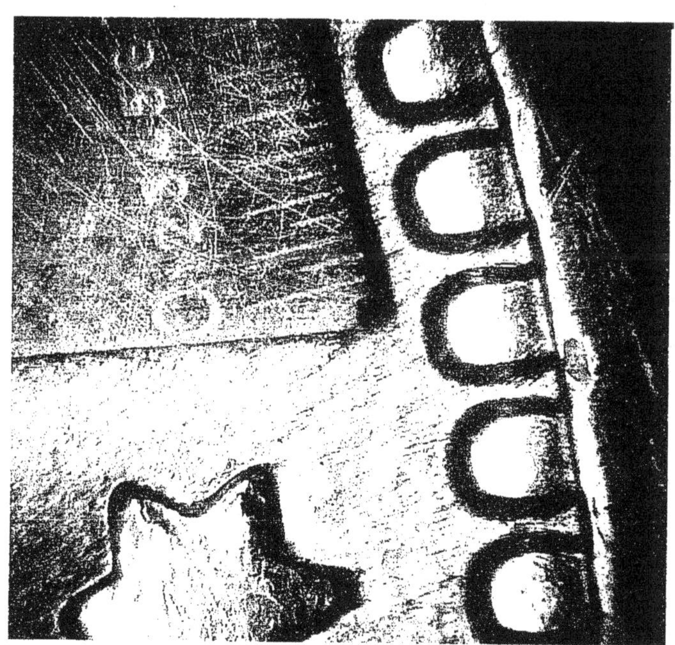

1902 O Distance Between Denticle Spaces 0.030"

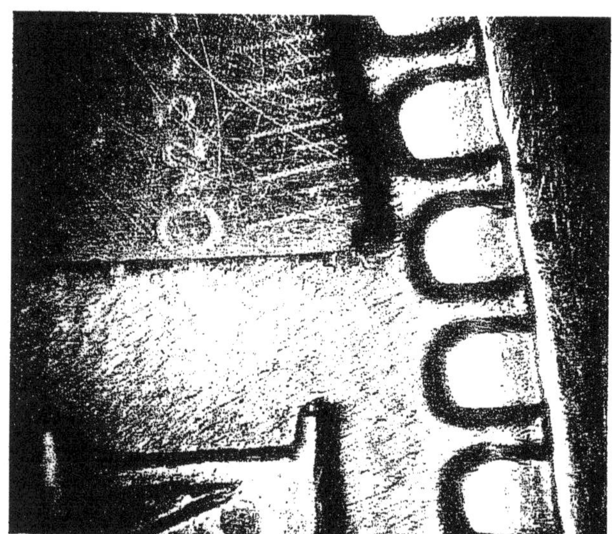

1902 O Denticle Space Width, 2 Triangles 0.005"

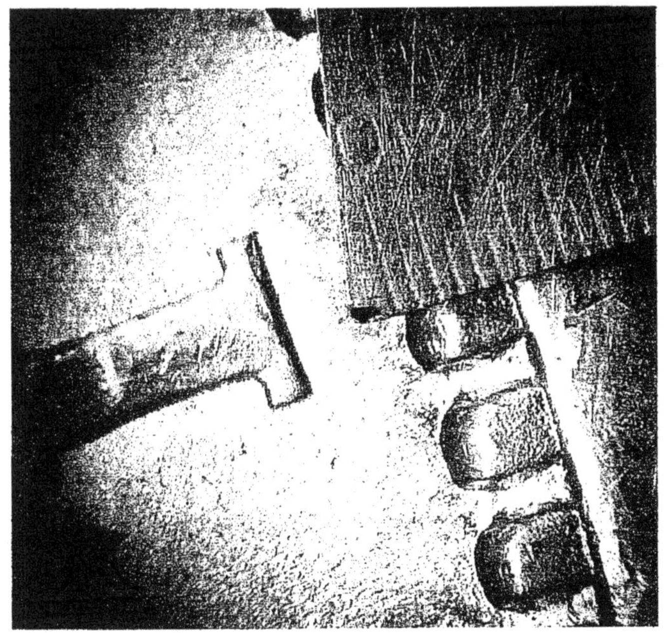

1921 P Denticle Length 0.025"

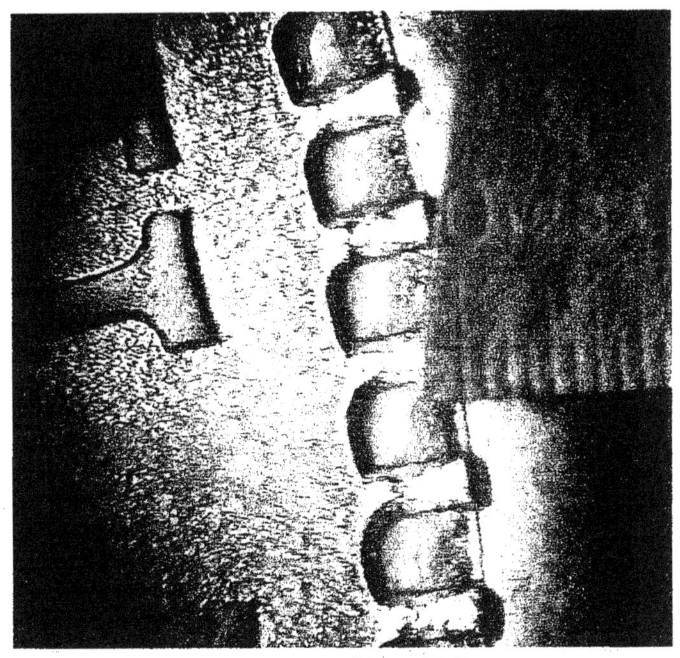

1921 P Rim Width 0.025"

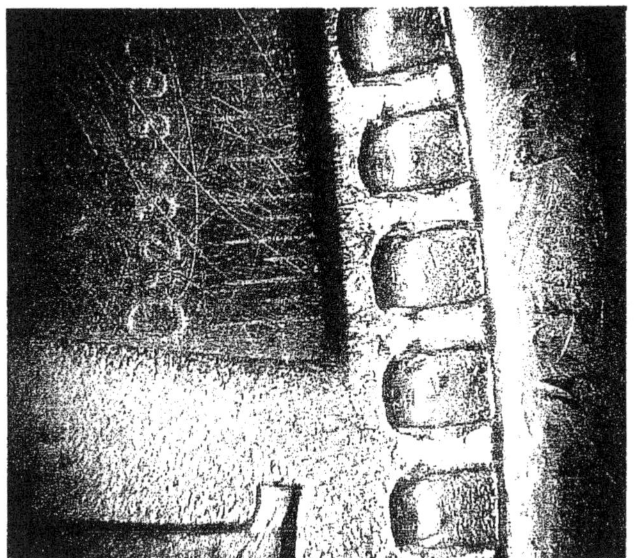

1921 P Denticle Width 0.020"

1921 P Distance Between Denticle Spaces 0.030"

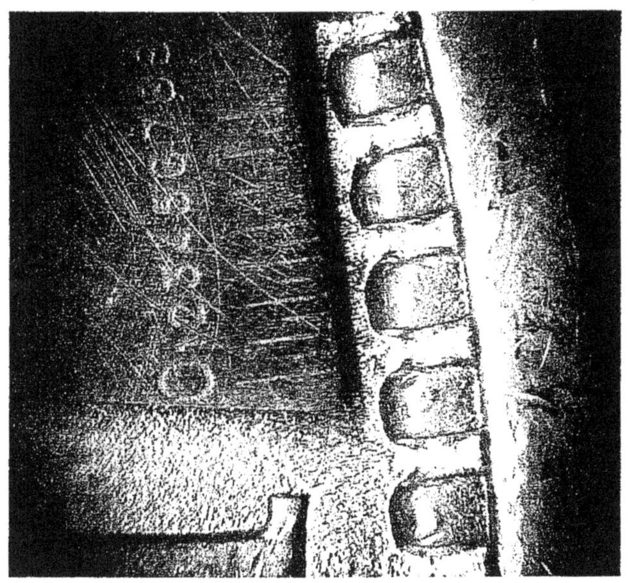

1921 P Denticle Space Width 0.010"

For these four coins the **denticle thicknesses were 0.007"- 0.008"** and **rim thicknesses were 0.010"**. Thus, the **denticle tops below the rim top were 0.002" to 0.003"**. These rim measurements were all for coins struck with basined and polished working dies and not of dies before basining. But they likely **approximate** the height measurements before basining.

These measurements are summarized in two separate sketches that show the side view of the rim, denticle and denticle space dimensions. A separate sketch shows a top view of rim depression, denticles depression and denticle space dimensions and shapes. These sketches are all for an **un-basined and un-polished die.**

Date Digit and Mint Mark Height Measurements

Since the caliper with 0.001" accuracy and 0.020" spacers were available, the thickness of the date digits and mint marks were measured for future study, such as how overdates and over mint marks were made.

Because the date digits are opposite the letters STATES on the reverse and the mint marks are opposite the wheat leaves and kernels on the obverse, a different measuring procedures was used. The digits and wheat leaves and kernels on the obverse and the letters and mint marks on the reverse are all of unknown height and may be different. The average of obv and reverse thickness of letters could not be used. Therefore, a fairly thin 0.020" plastic sheet that was rigid was placed against the coin reverse. A thin 0.020" thick spacer was placed above the digits in the field to obtain a relative nearby coin field, spacer and plastic sheet thickness measurement using the caliper. A similar setup was used to measure the combined thickness of the coin date, spacer and plastic sheet at the date digits but with a slightly wider spacer to cover the full digits height.

The date digit thickness was then obtained by subtracting the combined thickness of coin, spacer and plastic sheet at the field from the thickness of the coin, spacer and plastic sheet at the date. Coins measured were 1878 S, 1886 P, 1901 O, 1902 O and 1921 P. A **consistent date thickness of 0.005"** was obtained with only one coin slightly thicker at 0.006".

A similar set-up was used to measure the mint mark thickness. A 0.020" cardboard spacer with double stick tape on one side was placed on top of the mint mark and on the adjacent field. A thin rigid plastic sheet of 0.020" thickness was placed flat against the obverse side of the coin. The combined thickness of coin at mint mark and field, spacer and bottom plastic sheet was measured at the mint mark and adjacent field to the left using the caliper. The mint mark thickness was obtained by subtracting the total thickness measurement at the field from the total thickness measurement at the mint mark. Coins measured were 1878 S, 1901 O and 1902 O. **All three mint marks measured 0.004" thickness.**

Of course the date digits and mint marks thickness varied on Morgan dollar dies and coins because of the variations in depths punched into the working dies by hand. They could also be reduced in thickness in varying degrees from the basining and polishing the working dies received at each mint prior to being installed in the coining presses, plus later polishing to remove die clash marks, die cracks and die pitting. A **likely range of thickness** may be **0.004"- 0.007" for the date digits** and **0.003"- 0.005" for the mint marks**.

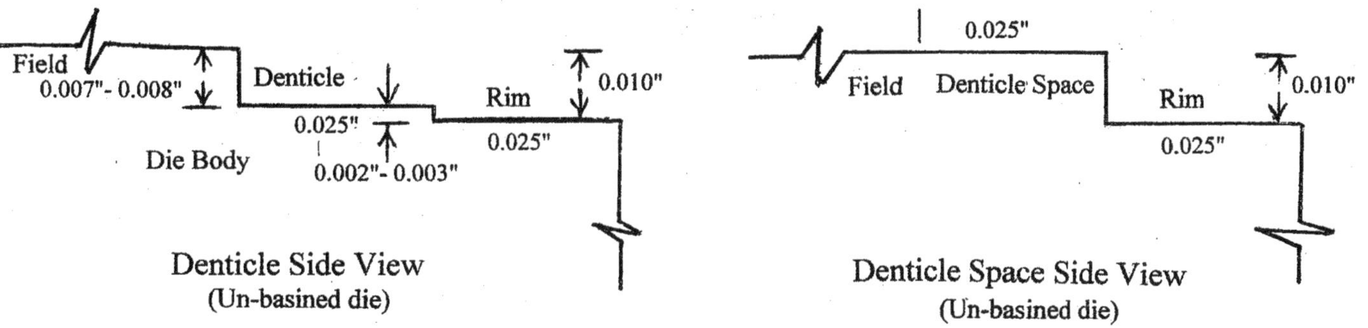

Denticle Side View
(Un-basined die)

Denticle Space Side View
(Un-basined die)

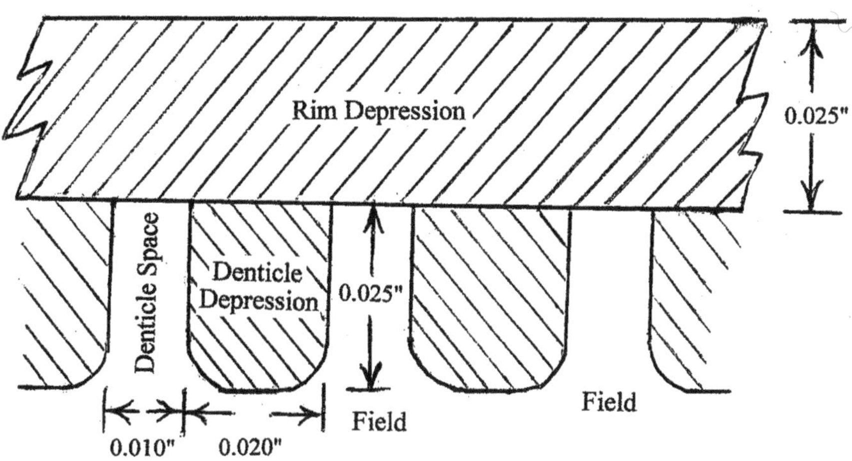

Rim, Denticle & Space Top View
(Un-basined die)

DIE BASINING AND POLISHING EFFECTS

The Morgan dollar working dies **usually did not** have the denticle spaces that were **flat at the field level** and **rectangular in shape**. Also the denticles usually were not a depressed rectangle with straight sides in the working dies. The close-up photographs in the previous chapter of the 1878 CC die face show over-polished denticles and denticle spaces on the right side of the die (left side of a struck coin). On the left side of the die, the denticle depressions are somewhat enlarged and the denticles spaces are narrowed with wedge of triangle shapes.

Die basining and polishing of the 1878 CC die caused these changes in the denticles and denticle spaces shape. They were performed on the working dies at each mint before they were installed in the coining presses.

Die basining was briefly described in the Neil Shafer article, *The Morgan Silver Dollars 1878-1921*, The Whitman Numismatic Journal, November 1964. It was a process of a fixture holding the die face against a slowly revolving dish shaped zinc lap eight inches in diameter and one and one half inches thick. A fine lens grinding compound and water on the lap polished the die face to a **specific radius of curvature**. Typically the radius was different for the obverse and reverse of Morgan working dies and sometimes varied for different types of coining presses. The purpose of the die basining was to cause the planchet metal flow when struck by the die **to evenly fill up** the die cavities from die center all way to the rim. This was not always accomplished as O mint coins typically had weak centers and S mint coins had full centers and weak rims.

Letters in the VAM book mention basin and their problems of Engraver George Morgan to Director of the Mint Dr. Henry Linderman on March 26 and May 17, 1878; Chief Engraver Charles Barber to Superintendent of the Philadelphia Mint James Pollock on about March 13, 1878; Coiner O.C. Bosbyshell to Pollack on April 1, 1878; and in 1880 from the then Superintendent of the Philadelphia Mint, Colonel Loudon Snowden to the new Director of the Mint Burchard that mentions basining difficulties in 1878.

Measurements of Coin Field Height Changes From Basining

The change of the field thickness from about the coin center to near the rim was measured using a caliper and 0.020" spacers procedures as described in the previous chapter. The Morgan dollar coin obverse does not have a field near the coin center as it is taken up by the Liberty head portrait. For the coin reverse, the closest field area to the coin center large enough to place spacers is that between the eagle's head and the eagle's right shoulder.

A flat rigid plastic of 0.020" thickness was placed flat against the obverse of a coin. Spacers of 0.020" thickness with double stick tape on one side were placed at the eagle's right shoulder field and the field between ES of STATES and OF near the denticles. The caliper measured the total thickness of the flat plastic sheet against the obverse, coin thickness and spacers at the two field locations. Subtracting these total measured thicknesses gave the change of field height due to any initial field curvature of the working die due to hubbing and the later die basining at each mint. Any initial field curvature on the working die is not known, so the field height change measurements is a **total** of the **initial die hubbed radius** and later **basining radius**.

Six coins were measured for this change of field height from near the coin center to near the denticles: 1878 S B^1 reverse, 1878 S B^2 reverse, 1883 P, 1883 O, 1890 P and 1902 O. Four coins measured an 0.005" field height change, the 1883 O 0.006" and the 1890 P 0.004". The **average reverse field change of 0.005"** if caused by just the die basining at the mints would have likely reduced the peripheral design considerably which is not evident on the coins. So the change of field height must be a **combination** of the **hubbing field curvature** and **mint die basining**.

Denticle Space Changes From Die Basining

Denticle spaces project from the **un-basined and polished** working dies as **flat rectangles projections** of 0.025" long, 0.010" wide and 0.008" high. Their ends are next to the 0.010" deep rim **depression** and their sides are above the 0.008" deep denticles **depressions**. They are the **highest and furthest out die projections** to the working die rim depression during the die basining and polishing. An accompany sketch illustrates these **vulnerable** denticle space projections out above the denticle depressions ending at the rim depression. Thus, they are **tiny 0.025" long, 0.010" wide and 0.008" thick projections** exposed the die basining grinding compound and flexible polishing wheel with compound. It did not take much basining and polishing to **deform** them significantly.

Morgan **proof dies** generally had only struck about 600-1,200 coins each year. So their dies did not experience much wear in striking the proof coins. The accompanying photographs of **proof** 1883, two 1885, 1886, 1887, 1888 and 1904 coin denticles **all show** most of the denticle spaces raised from the die basining and polishing and not flat rectangles. They generally show short flat shaped triangles inner ends at the field level with longer narrowed raised outer sections with sloping sides. This corresponds to polished down denticle spaces on the working dies caused by the die basining and polishing.

A photograph of EDS PL 1878 S VAM 26 shows wedge shaped inner denticle spaces ends with sloping outer portion on the obverse and some flat wide over-polished denticles and spaces on the reverse. Thus, the die basining and polishing sometimes affected the die denticle spaces differently for the obverse and reverse dies.

Photographs of both the obverse and reverse denticle spaces for an EDS PL 1881 O VAM 53 with little die wear show triangular inner and outer ends of the denticle spaces. The obverse photograph of an 1881 O VAM 54 EDS DMPL shows short triangular inner denticle spaces and shallow narrow outer denticle spaces.

Other coin photographs of 1879 P, 1887 P, 1888 S, 1889 P and 1890 O show short triangular inner denticle spaces and various outer ends of polished shapes of rectangular, narrow with sloping sides and wedge shaped. An 1878 S VAM 17 photograph shows over polished wide rectangular flat denticle spaces on the obverse.

These photographs of coins show that die basining and polishing of the working dies **often polished the outer two-thirds of the denticle spaces** into **depressed sloping areas** with **blunt ends** at the rim depression and **sloping sides** of various shapes at the denticle depressions. The shorter one-third of the **inner denticle spaces** near the flat field were often **triangle or wedge shaped** at the same level as the field. This made the inner denticle spaces **higher** than the outer beveled portion of the denticle spaces **on the dies**. The inner part of the denticles spaces were exposed and **more likely to contact** an opposing reverse die field to create the raised triangles of denticle impressions as the dies were being installed in the coining presses.

These changes in denticle space shapes are illustrated in the accompanying sketches. A **side view** depicts the rounded polished denticle space that ends at the rim depression. The other end of the denticle space remains at the field level. An **end view** of the denticle space projections show a depressed and rounded narrow end at the rim depression.

A **top view** sketch of the denticle spaces, denticle depressions and rim depression depicts depressed denticle space about two-thirds of the distance from the rim depression, triangle or wedge shaped inner ends at the same level as the field and polished sloping sides going into the denticle depressions. These depicted denticle space inner and outer end shapes are consistent with those seen on numerous coin examples and of denticle impressions on many coin reverse fields.

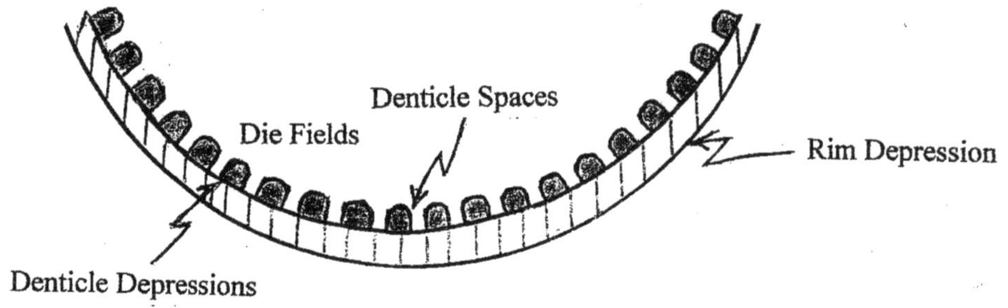

Denticle Space Projections
(Un-basined die)

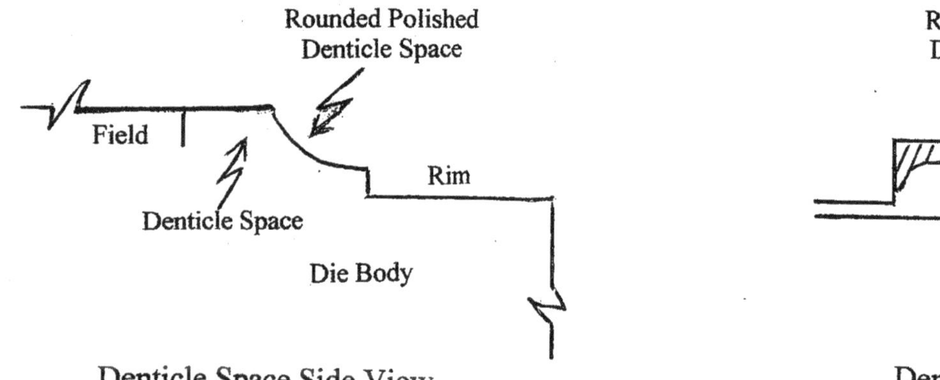

Denticle Space Side View
(Polished denticle space)

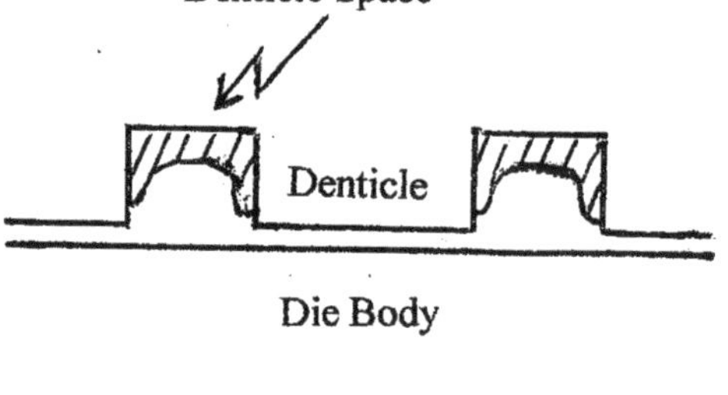

Denticle Space End View
(Polished denticle Spaces)

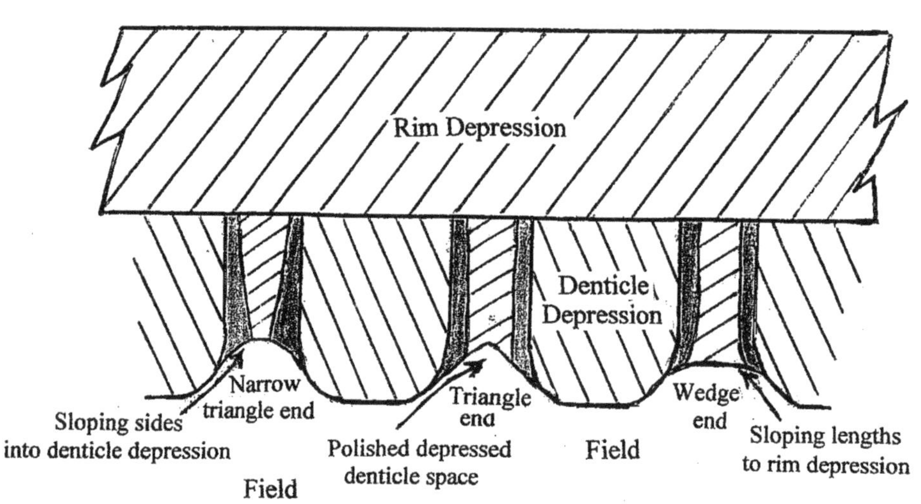

Basining of Die Causing Polished Depressed Denticle Space

1883 Proof VAM 22 Doubled 3, Triangular Denticle Spaces

1885 Proof VAM 31 Doubled 85, Triangular Denticle Spaces

1885 Proof VAM 38 Triangular Denticle Spaces, Obv

1885 Proof VAM 38 Triangular Denticle Spaces, Rev

1886 Proof VAM 15 Triangular & Narrow Denticle Spaces

1887 Proof VAM 32 Doubled 7, Triangular Denticle Spaces

1888 Proof VAM 25 Doubled Date, Triangular Denticle Spaces

1904 Proof VAM 8 Triangular Denticle Spaces

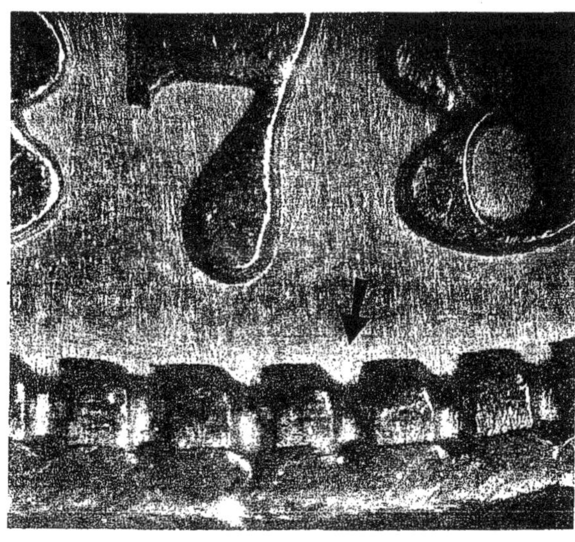
1878 S VAM 26 Wedge Denticle Spaces, EDS PL

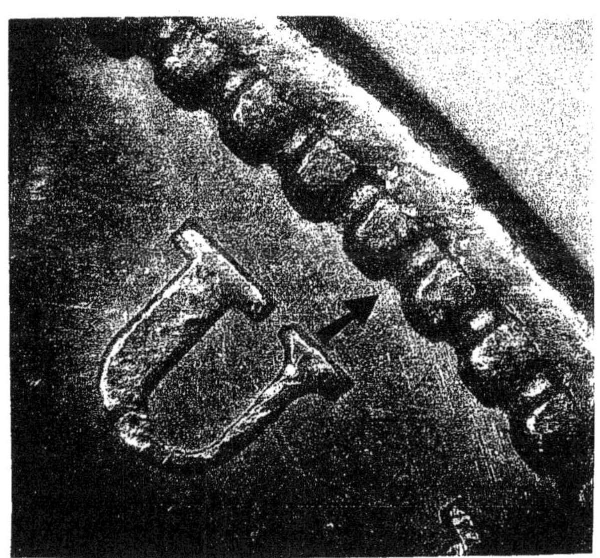
1878 S VAM 26 Obv Wedge Denticle Spaces, Sloping Outer Portion EDS PL

1878 S VAM 26 Rev Flat Wide Denticle Spaces, EDS PL, Slightly Over Polished

1878 S VAM 26 Rev Deep Narrow Denticle Spaces, Slight Slope, EDS PL

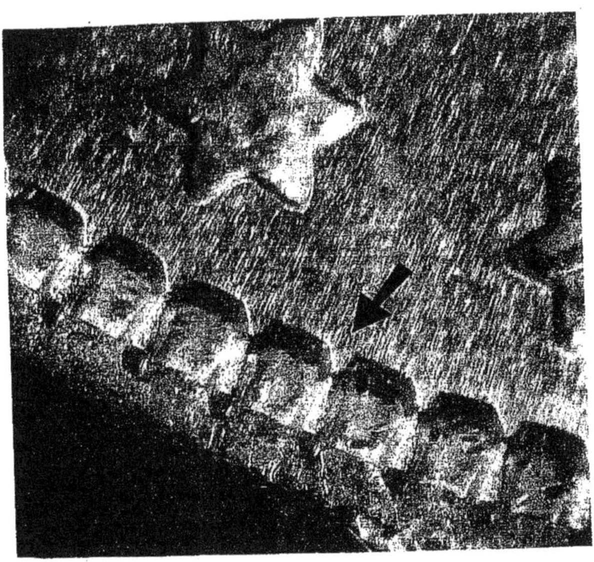

1881 O VAM 53 Obv Triangular Denticle Spaces, EDS PL

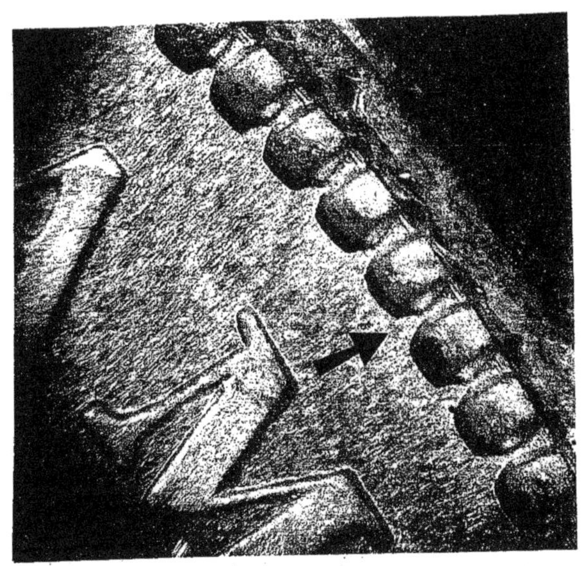

1881 O VAM 53 Rev Triangular Denticle Spaces, EDS PL

1881 O VAM 54 Obv Triangular Denticle Spaces Inner, Shallow Narrow Outer, EDS DMPL

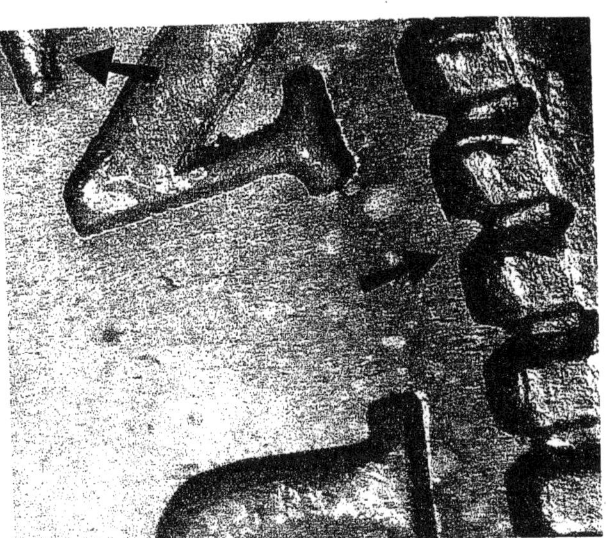

1879 P VAM 36 Obv Triangular & Shallow Wedge Denticle Spaces

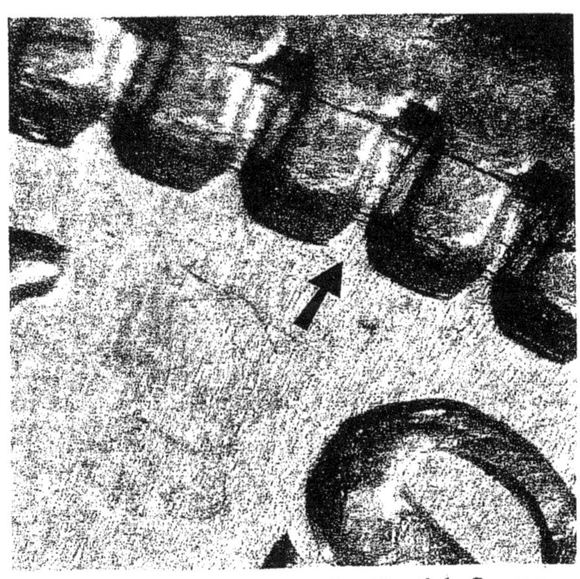

1879 P VAM 67 Obv Wedge Denticle Spaces, Polishing Lines

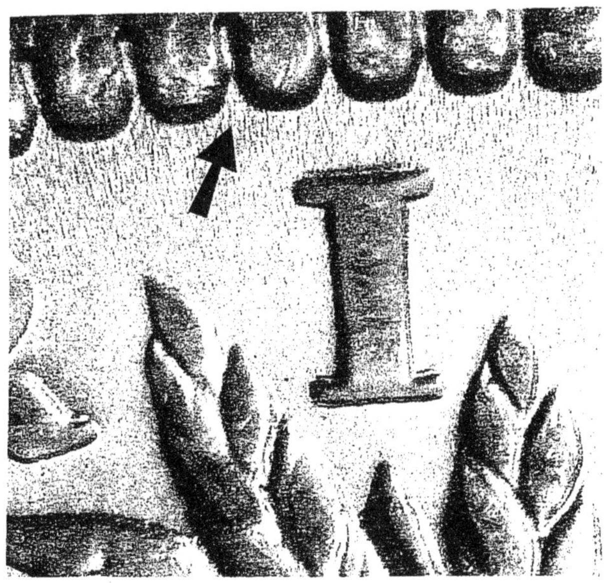

1887 P VAM 15 Obv Triangular & Narrow Denticle Spaces

1888 S VAM 3C Obv Rounded & Narrow Triangle Denticle Spaces

1889 P VAM 62 Triangular & Rectangular Denticle Spaces

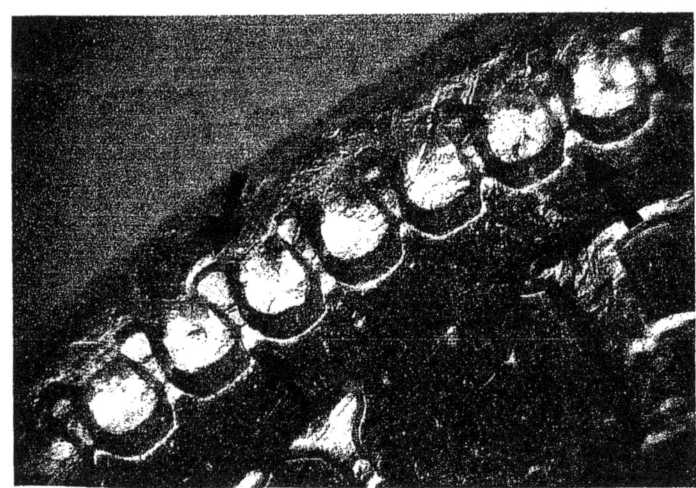

1890 O VAM 1C Obv Triangular, Some Damaged Denticle Spaces

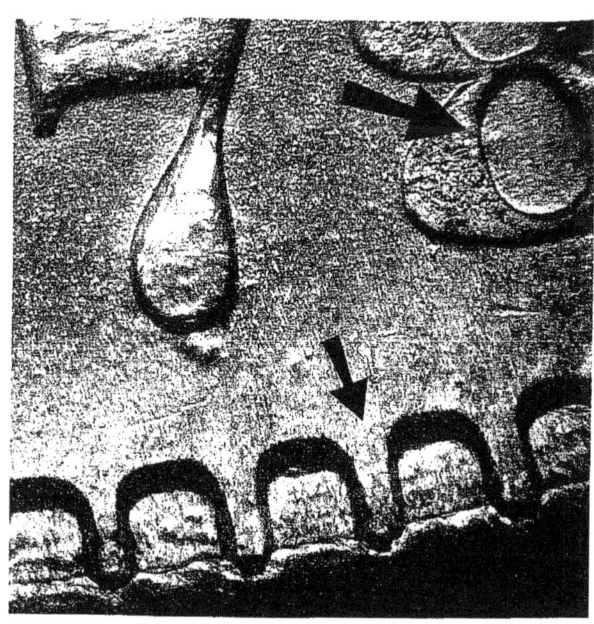

1878 S VAM 17 Over Polished Wide Rectangular Denticle Spaces

HOW DENTICLE SPACE IMPRESSIONS HAPPENED

Dozens of Morgan reverse dies show small raised dots various shapes in the fields. They have been found on most of the years from 1878 thru 1921 of the Morgan dollar production. They have been reported for most of the mints that struck the Morgan dollar including the Philadelphia, New Orleans, San Francisco, Carson City but not yet 1921 Denver Mint so far.

These raised dots are found in a slightly curved line with a spacing of 0.030" between the dots. The curvature closely matches the size of the circular die face of the 1.5" diameter for Morgan dollars.

It is unlikely that a special tool used on the coining presses accidentally made the impressions into the dies since no common tool is known to have these sharp edges with this spacing. Reeding on the edge of the coins have similar spacing, but not exactly since the edge reeding count and spacing varied over the span of Morgan dollar production and at each mint. Besides, the reeding is inside the circular collars and could not impact the flat fields of the dies.

The spacing of the raised dots in the reverse die fields exactly match the 0.030" denticle spacing as determined in the chapter, Anatomy of Morgan Dollar Die. Therefore, the simple logical cause of the raised dots is the accidental impact of the obverse denticle spaces at the die edge into the field of another reverse die.

Denticle spaces on the basined and polished Morgan dollar dies had various shapes as shown in the previous chapter, Die Basining And Polishing Effects. The inner and outer ends of basined and polished denticle spaces typically were triangle or wedge shaped. Other shapes include rounded dots and sometimes in rare cases rather flat short rectangles of lightly basined or over polished dies. They always have a spacing between these shapes of 0.030" of denticle spaces separation as shown in the chapter, Anatomy of Morgan Dollar Die.

Possible Ways Dies Contacted

The obvious next question is how would the dies accidently come into contact to produce the denticle space impressions? Working dies would normally be well protected when in storage or in transit to another mint. Contemporary dies usually have a plastic cap that fits tightly over a greased or oiled die face for protection and to keep it from rusting. Morgan dollar dies would have had oil or grease on the die face and perhaps a fabric or leather cap for protection. The Morgan dollar dies would have been stored or transported upright in compartmented wooden boxes to keep the die separated.

The most likely place for a die edge to contact another die's field would be in the coining press. An accompanying photograph shows the No. 1 coining press that was used to strike Morgan dollars at the Carson City Mint. A close-up photograph shows the die chamber of this No. 1 press. There is very little vertical space in which to install the obverse and reverse dies. For the Morgan dollars, the **upper hammer die was the obverse die** as evidenced by partial collar coins with the partial reeding of the collar always showing next to the reverse of the coin with the railroad smooth rim that was above the collar next to the coin obverse. (See pages 62 and 134 in the VAM book for description of the coining press and photographs of the partial collar Morgan dollar coins.)

Another photograph shows the upper dies and feed fingers of a 1970s dual coining press with a close-up of the die chamber also shown with the upper die shown on the right side. The dies frequently clashed while operating in the presses but only the flat die faces came together and not the edge of a die.

A possible explanation of how the dies might have impacted in the coining presses is that it happened during the installation of removal of the dies. If **during the installation or removal of the upper die** from a press the workman **accidently contacted the exposed lower reverse die face**, the denticle space edge and/or the die edge could have been transferred. The vertical space between the obverse and reverse dies in the press was very short. Both the obverse ans reverse dies were in a hardened state during their installation in the coining presses. Any brush, tick or drop of the tilted

No. 1 Press For Carson City Mint

Feed Fingers & Upper Dies in Press 1970s

Die Chamber No. 1 Press For Carson City Mint

upper obverse die could have caused the denticle and/or die edge impressions on the lower reverse die fields.

Denticle Spaces Actually Made Impressions

Because the dies were hardened when they were used in the coining presses, it would take another piece of hardened steel to make much of an impression on a die. The opposite die in a coining press was hardened steel that could make such an impression into the field of a die.

Since the space between the denticles is raised on the die in order to impress it **into** the coin, the denticle shapes are recessed on the die to make them **raised** on the coin. Thus, it is actually the obverse die **space edge between the denticles** that contacted a reverse die field and cause raised triangle dot impressions.

In some cases, the impact of the obverse die edge onto the reverse die field damaged the denticle spaces somewhat flattening them. A prime example is the 1878 S VAM 17A for the denticle spaces above R and BU in PLURIBUS respectively. Note that some of the denticle spaces have been pushed up on the coin at the rear near the rim and lengthened towards the coin center near the field. The rest of the adjacent denticle spaces appear normally recessed. This indicates that the obverse denticle spaces opposite the denticle impressions at OLL and below the tail feathers were the ones that contacted the reverse die field and were slightly deformed because of the dies impacting..

Another photograph shows the double row of denticle impressions below the arrow and tail feathers for the 1890 O VAM 1C. The accompanying photograph shows some damaged denticle spaces on the 1890 O VAM 1C coin obverse at UR in PLURIBUS that have been pushed up like those on the 1878 S VAM 17A. It is apparent that the damaged denticle spaces near the rim could have produced the lower row of reverse rounded end denticle impressions of the 1890 O VAM 1C and the denticle spaces near the field of triangular shape could have made the upper row of reverse triangular shape denticle impressions, with spacing between the rows of the denticle spaces length.

As discussed and shown in the chapter, Die Basining and Polishing effects, the denticle spaces could have various shapes on a basined and polished die. The severity of the basining and polishing varied with the dies because it was controlled by the mint operator. As a result, the denticle spaces were most frequently at a polished angle from the field. Plus, the outer edge at the rim; cavity and the inner edge at the field adjacent to the denticle cavities varied in shape. The most common shapes were triangles and wedges. Others had more rounded shapes. A few had mostly flat nearly rectangular shape near the field level. Occasionally an over polished die had mostly rectangular denticle space shapes at the field level. But such severe over polished dies were somewhat rare instances.

Possible Obverse Die Contact Angles With Reverse Die

A separate sketch broadly shows the reverse die face retracted below the top of the surrounding collar. The upper obverse die is slightly tilted so it's die face is slightly above the collar and the opposite side is making contact with the lowered reverse die.

After the coin is struck, the obverse die is raised about half and inch. This allows the reverse die to then rise about one eighth of an inch slightly later. The press feed fingers then pushes the coin off the reverse die over the surrounding collar. (Source for these distances is, *Illustrated History of the U.S. Mint* by A. M. Smith, ed., Philadelphia, by editor, 1881 pg 26.)

The coin total thickness at the rim is the thickest part of the coin to allow even stacking of coins and to protect the devices. This total coin thickness at the rim was measured during the determination of the rim height above the coin field, as discussed in the chapter, Anatomy of Morgan Dollar Die. Ten coins of various dates and mint marks from 1878 to 1921 had an average total rim thickness of 0.110". So the lower die raising up one-eighth of an inch (0.0125") after the coin was struck was sufficient to allow the coin to be pushed off the lower die and over the collar top surface.

The separate diagram **to scale** shows about the minimum angle that the obverse die needs to be

1878 S VAM 17A Lengthened Denticle Spaces R

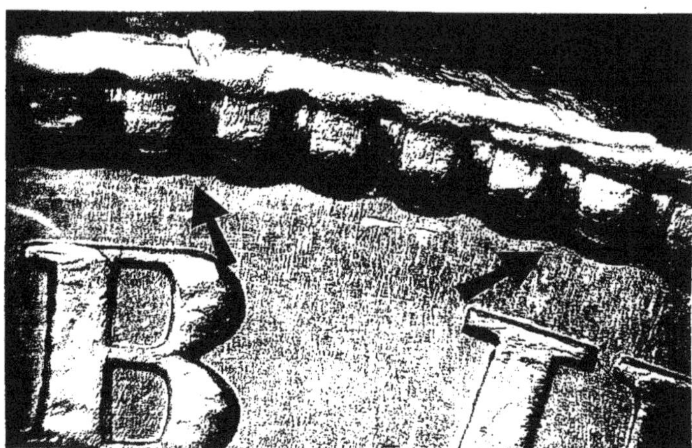

1878 S VAM 17A Lengthened Denticle Spaces BU

1890 O VAM 1C Denticle Impressions

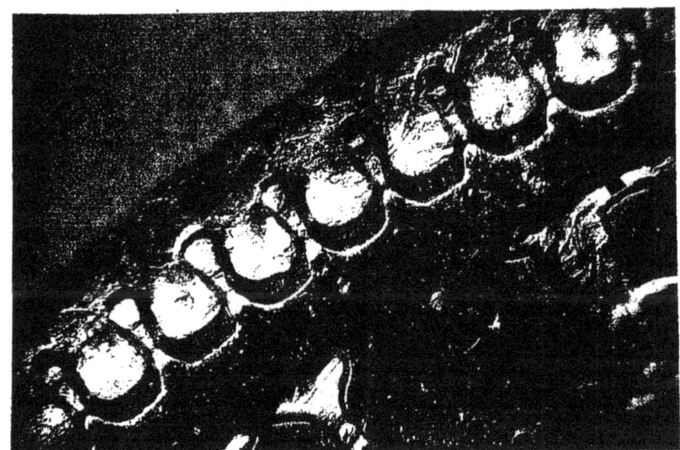

1890 O VAM 1C Obverse Denticle Spaces UR

Upper Dies in Press 1970s

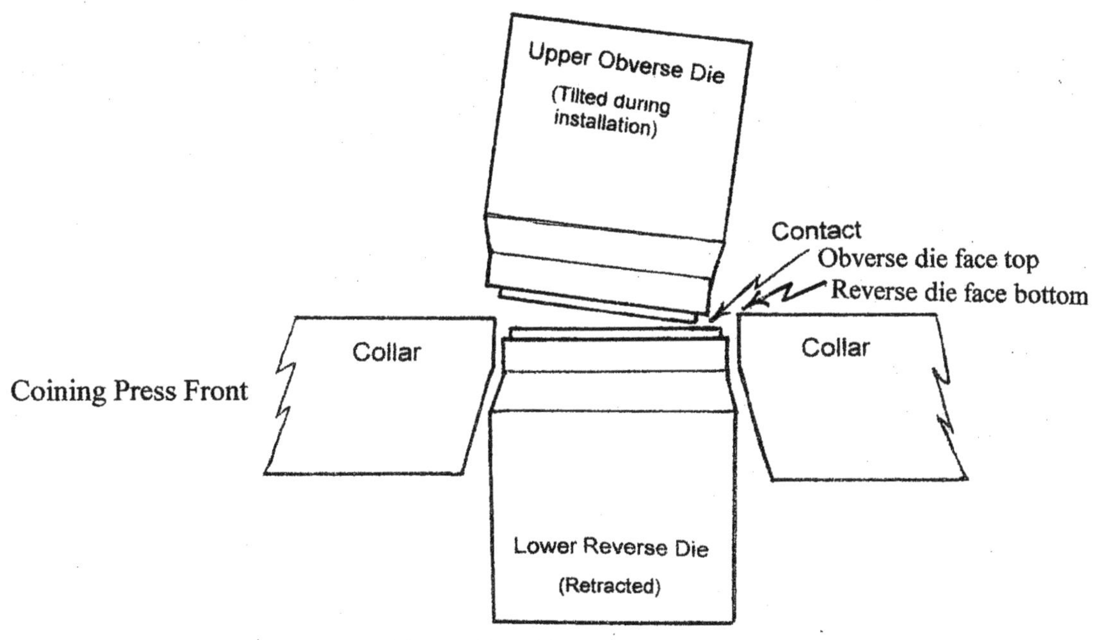

Upper Die Contact on Lower Die
(Press side view)

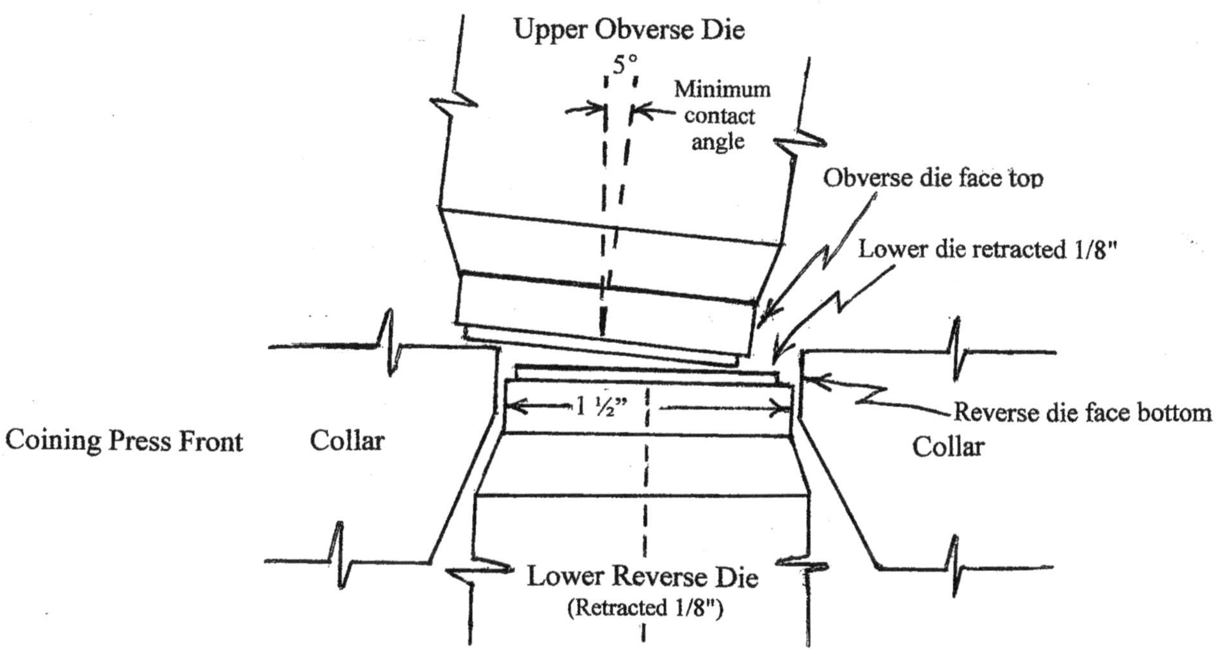

Minimum Contact Angle With Retracted Lower Die
(Actual size 1.5" die face diameter)
(Press side view)

tilted to clear the higher collar edge and have the upper obverse die top touch the lower die lower reverse. This angle is only about 5° from the vertical. Obverse die tilt angles greater than this allows easy contact at the top obverse die denticles with the flat fields of the lower reverse die. Thus, there is only a slight tilt of the upper obverse die for the obverse denticles to accidently make contact with the lower reverse die fields.

Position of Dies in Coining Presses

Most of the denticle impressions are below the eagle's tail feathers. Fewer occur below the wreath bow, at arrow feathers and below the arrow heads and wing lower edges. Die edge impressions and associated denticle impressions and possible die edge impressions alone are mostly at the lower reverse. Most of these impressions show a deeper edge of the denticle impression towards the lower reverse edge. Usually the top obverse die was positioned in the coining presses so the struck coin showed the obverse in the normal upright orientation as viewed by the coining press operator at the coining press front. Thus, the reverse die could have been placed up-side-down in the coining press relative to the coining press workman and was impressed with the obverse die top edge when it was accidently tilted forward away from the workman and down during the installation of the upper obverse die. Cases of opposite obverse die tilt contact also occurred.

Possible Ways Denticle Space and Rim Edges Could Contact Die Reverse Fields

The accompanying sketches depict the **three possible obverse die contacts** on the reverse die field when the denticle spaces are **not polished.** If the flat denticle space end above the rim depression only contacted the reverse die field, it would cause a flat ended wedge depression. At an angle of about 22° from the die axis vertical, both the denticle space end and rim depression outside edge would simultaneously contact the reverse die field. The wedge shaped denticle space ends would be about 0.027" away from the slightly curved die edge line. Beyond the 22° from die axis vertical, only the die edge would contact the reverse die fields producing a slightly curved die impression which would be a raised curved line on a coin. These raised curved lines of the rim edge impression are evident on a number of Morgan dollar reverse dies and Peace dollar obverse dies.

The unpolished obverse die denticle space ends contact with the Morgan dollar reverse die is likely a **fairly rare occurrence**, as most coin obverses show polished denticle spaces of various shapes. Also, most reported denticle space impressions on coin reverses show the shapes of the polished ends of the inner end of the denticle spaces. These most often appear as **raised triangles** on the denticle impressions on coin reverses. Other shapes of denticle impressions are raised wedges, rounded dots, half moon with straight edge and rarely as flat partial rectangles. These various denticle impression shapes were caused by variations in the degree of basining and polishing of the denticle space projections on the working dies obverses.

The accompanying sketches shows **some possible ways** the obverse die with polished denticle spaces could contact the reverse die field. Assuming a typical unpolished denticle space length of about **one-third at the die field end**, this portion of the denticle space could contact the reverse die field at about 1° to 12° die axis from the vertical. This polished inner edge of the denticle space and outer rim edge could **simultaneously** contact the reverse die field at angles of about 12° to 18° depending on the length of the unpolished denticle space segment. The distance of unpolished segment contact triangles or wedge impressions from the slightly curved rim edge impression would be about 0.025" to 0.045" depending upon the length of the unpolished segment.

Another possible way the denticle space and outside of the rim edge could contact the reverse die field would be for the **denticle space front edge** at the rim depression and the outside rim edge simultaneously contact the reverse die field. It could happen for the die axis to be about 12° to 22° from the vertical depending upon the severity of the polished outside end of the denticle spaces as illustrated in accompanying sketch. Such simultaneous contact of the denticle space outside end and rim outside edge would produce denticle impressions triangles with a **flat side towards** the slightly curved rim impression about 0.025" to 0.027" distance away.

Some simultaneous contacts of the outer denticle space end with well defined line of straight triangle bases and dots of the inner denticle space about 0.025" directly above the triangle also occur. A few rare occurrences show the slightly curved outside rim impression with a row of triangles 0.025" above the line of the outside denticle space ends and another row of dots about 0.020" above the triangles from the inside denticle space impression.

The curved line of the rim outside edge impression could occur **alone** sometimes at 12° to 22° die axis from the vertical, depending upon the extent of the polished down denticle space end. It would **always show alone** beyond 22° die axis from the vertical if the obverse die contacted the reverse die field..

All the denticle space inside and outside die impressions are **spaced 0.030" apart**. They are on a **slightly curved radius** like the rim die edge impressions. However, about four or more spaced denticle impressions in a line are needed to see much of a curve.

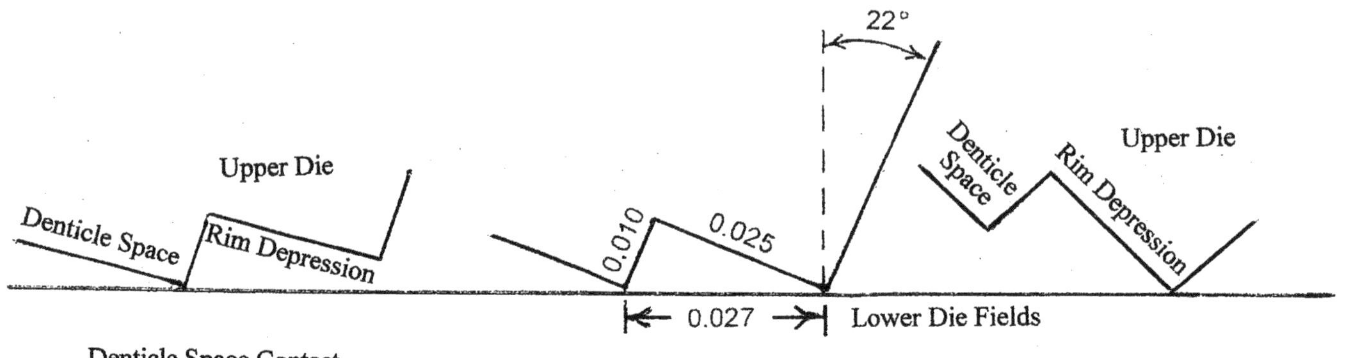

Possible Die Edge & Denticle Space Contacts
(Denticle space not polished)

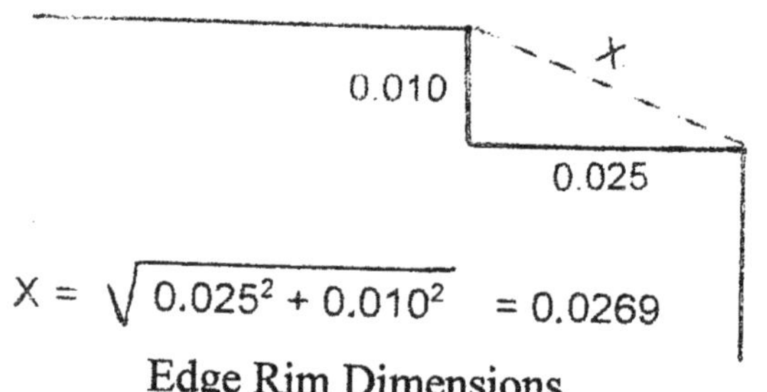

Edge Rim Dimensions

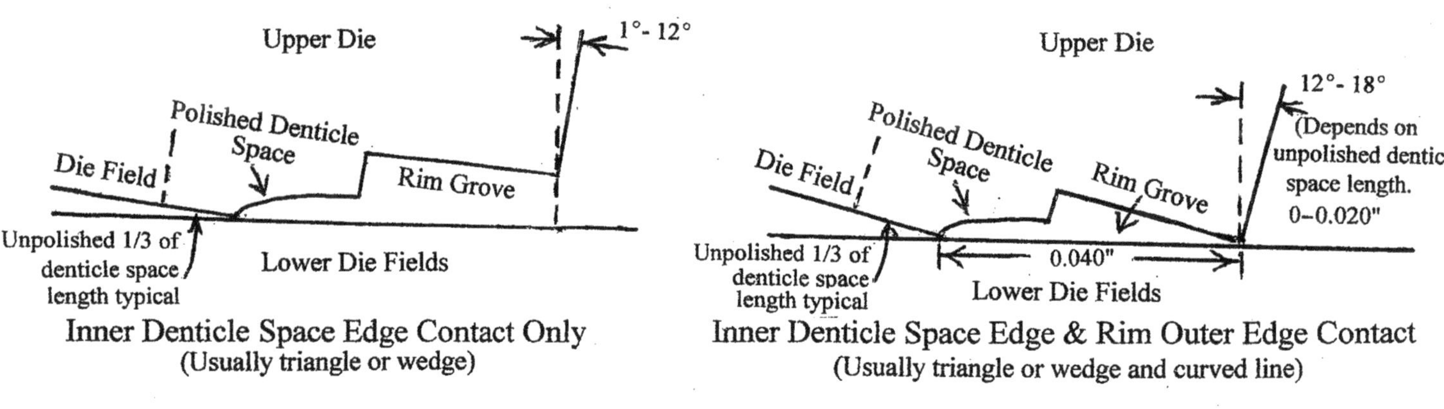

Inner Denticle Space Edge Contact Only
(Usually triangle or wedge)

Inner Denticle Space Edge & Rim Outer Edge Contact
(Usually triangle or wedge and curved line)

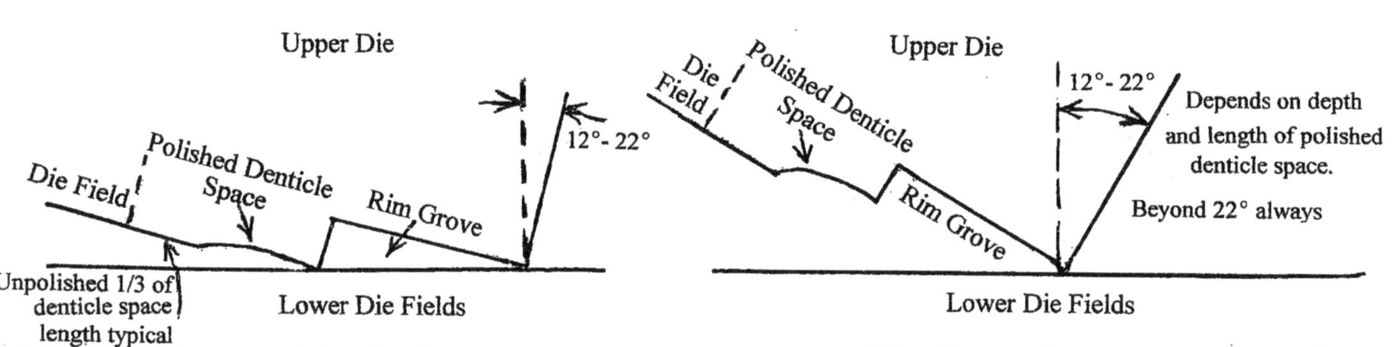

Outer Denticle Space Edge & Rim Outer Edge Contact
(Wedge and curved line)

Rim Outer Edge Contact Only
(Single curved line)

MEASURING DENTICLE IMPRESSION SPACES

Raised dots or triangles in a line on a coin **need to be checked for the spacing distance** between them to see if the distance matches that of the denticle spacing of 0.030" near the rim. This denticle spacing was shown in the previous chapter, Anatomy of Morgan Dollar Dies. A single raised bump or dot can seldom be confirmed as a denticle impression because die chips frequently occur on the Morgan dollar dies. Some exceptions are the 1886 O VAM 1C that has a **single large raised triangle** dot below the right tail feather and the 1904 O VAMs 12/22A with a similar looking **large raised triangle dot** below the eagle's right wing next to the leg feathers. These two large triangles have sharp outlines that are not typical of the ragged edges of various shapes of die chips.

Generally, it is best to have three or more raised dots in a line in order to double check that the spacing between them matches the denticle spacing. There are several cases however, that show only two raised triangle shapes that have bold outlines and deep impressions with easily measured spacing between the dots of the correct 0.030" denticle spacing, i.e., 1901 O VAM 45, 1921 P VAMs 3ER & 31B and 1921 S VAM 1AJ.

A convenient method to measure the raised dot spacing on a coin is to use a **mini-scale** designed for viewing under a microscope. An accompanying photograph shows one example of a mini-scale tool for microscopes with a flat scale at one end of a short rod with a small handle at the other end. The flat scale has divisions of 0.005" and numbers for each 0.01". Such measuring scales for microscopes can be obtained from laboratory supply firms. It's use was illustrated in the chapter Anatomy of Morgan Dollars.

A phtograph shows this scale near the obverse denticles of a 1902 O Morgan dollar. It can be seen that the **denticle spacing is 0.03"**. The same scale is shown next to the reverse denticles of the same 1902 O Morgan dollar and they have the **same spacing of 0.030"** as the obverse denticles. The **die edge is about 0.025"** beyond the denticle outside edge where the rim begins.

In the absence of a mini-scale tool, a simple **temporary scale** can be made on the **edge of a piece of white paper**. Place the straight edge of the paper near the denticles of a Morgan dollar. A fine line pencil can be used to make several short lines perpendicular to the paper edge at each denticle space or denticle, using a 7X of 10X hand glass or a 10X or 20X microscope. These marks will be of the 0.030" denticle spacing as shown in the accompanying photograph.

To measure the spacing between two or more raised dots on a coin, the mini-scale or paper scale is placed next to the row of raised dots. Because the mini-scale is a flat piece of metal with sharp edges and corners, it is best to place it on top of a flip or grading slab with the coin inside to protect it from potential scratches. The edge or point of the raised dots can be used as the measuring index to determine if the spacing is 0.030" of the denticle spacing when viewed with a 7X of 10X hand glass or 10X or 20X microscope.

An example of measuring denticle spacing is shown for the 1878 S VAM 17A reverse at OLL. In this case the denticle impressions have a broad rounded end and the left edge of the raised dot can be used as a reference point.

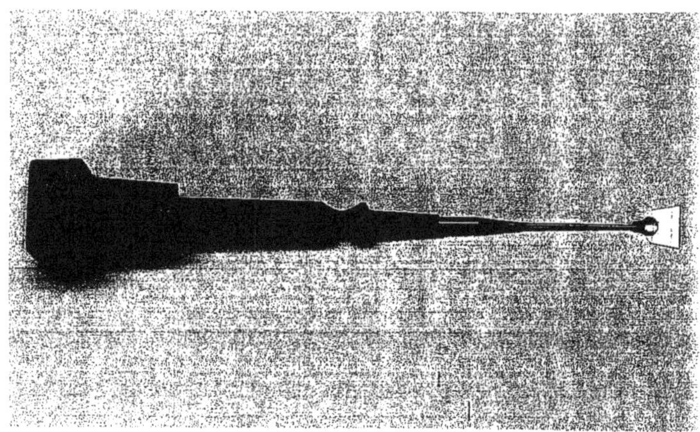

Mini-scale Tool for Microscopes

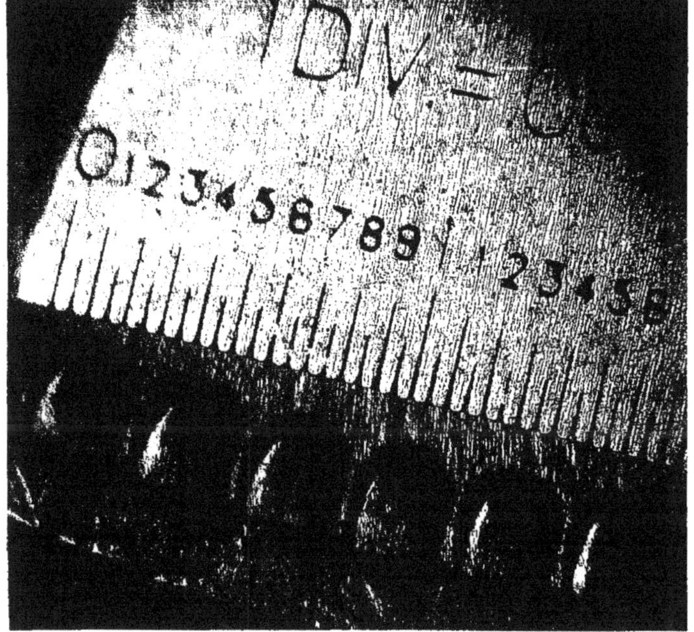

Obverse Denticle Spacing 0.03"

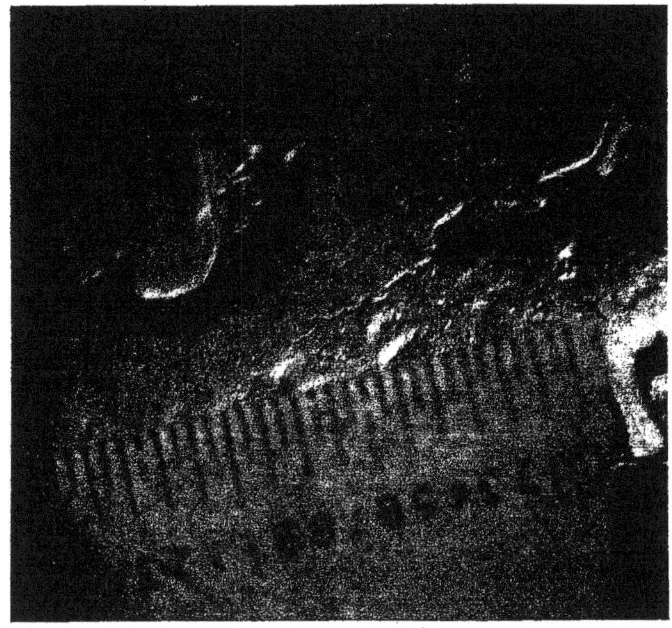

1878 S VAM 17C Measuring Denticle Impressions Spacing

Mini-scale for Microscopes

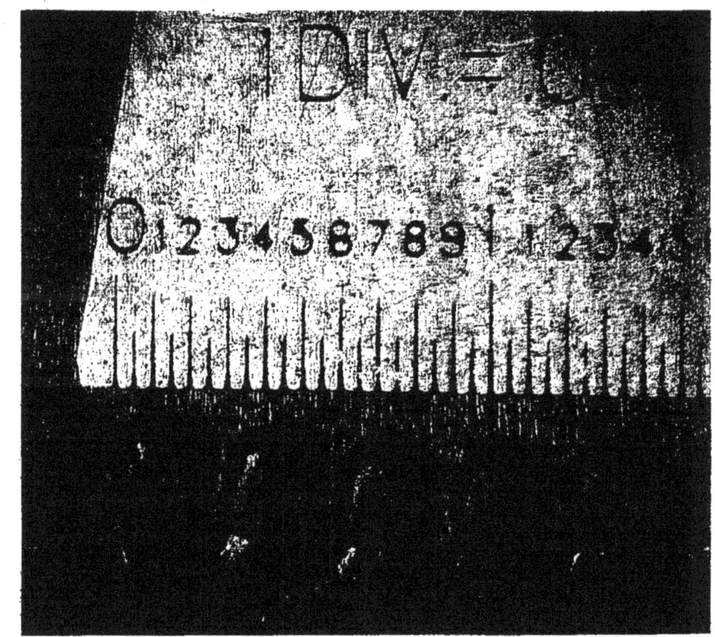

Reverse Denticle Spacing 0.03"

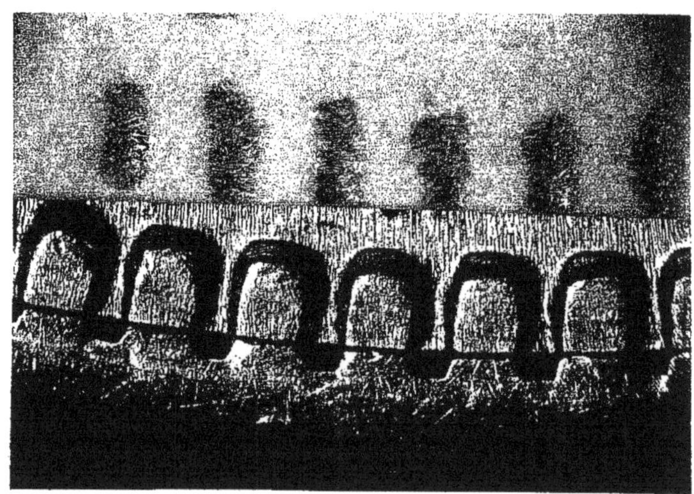

Denticle Spacing Marks on Paper Edge

QUICK ATTRIBUTION PHOTOGRAPHS

The following two sections show photographs of the denticle space impressions of the 19 new listings and a second section with previously listed denticle space impressions varieties. There are also five varieties that show die edge impressions along with the denticle space impressions as discussed in the chapters, **Types of Denticle Impressions** and **Types of Die Edge Impressions**. They are 1879 P VAM 57A, 1881 O VAM 18A, 1890 P VAM 1D, 1890 O VAM 1 I and 1921 S VAM 1AJ. The photographs can provide a ***quick comparison*** of an un-attributed denticle impressions variety coin with those that have been reported and listed to date.

These photographs also show the various shapes and strengths that the denticle space impressions have. Some are well defined triangles while others are wedge or crescent with blunt ends, and diffuse circle shapes. A few even have somewhat rounded ends. They can serve as a guide of what to look for when examining coins. But the **key** is the **same spacing of 0.030" between the dots in a line** as the denticles. Photographs of 22 possible examples of die edge impressions are shown in several sections of the chapter at the end of this document, **Photographs of Denticle & Die Edge Impressions**.

In some instances, namely the 1878 S VAMs 17A & B and 1904 O VAMs 12/22, several photographs show the change of the denticle impressions as the dies wore out or were polished. This is indicated by different die variety designations or die state designations.

On very shallow denticle impressions, the raised dots will tend to become fainter and more diffuse as the dies wore out. Thus, the photographs on the next pages can be used to confirm the exact placement of the raised dots for the listed known varieties. If the raised dots in a line on a coin don't match the listed varieties photographs, then it may be a new unlisted denticle impressions variety. The coin should then be sent to the author for examination and possible listing at the address shown in the **Introduction**.

GROUPED PHOTOGRAPHS OF NEW DENTICLE IMPRESSIONS

1878 S VAM 34A Three Denticle Impressions Rim- N of UNITED

1878 S VAM 34A Three Denticle Impressions Olive Leaf Cluster

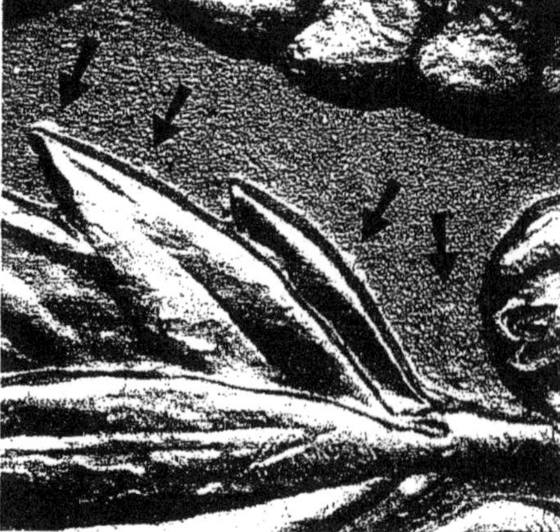
1884 P VAM 8J Denticle Impressions Leaf Edges

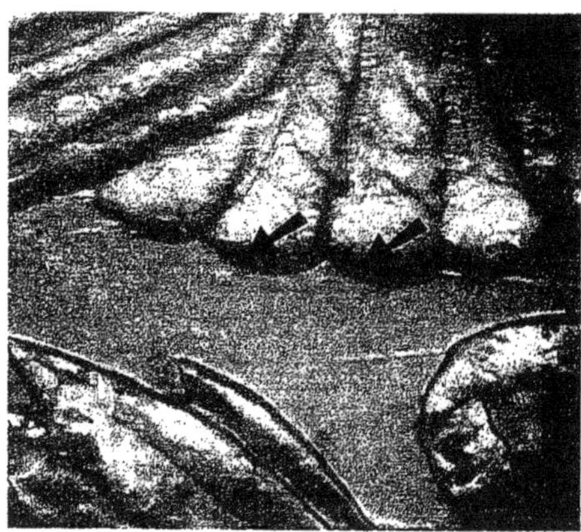
1889 P VAM 1C1 Denticle Impressions Below TF

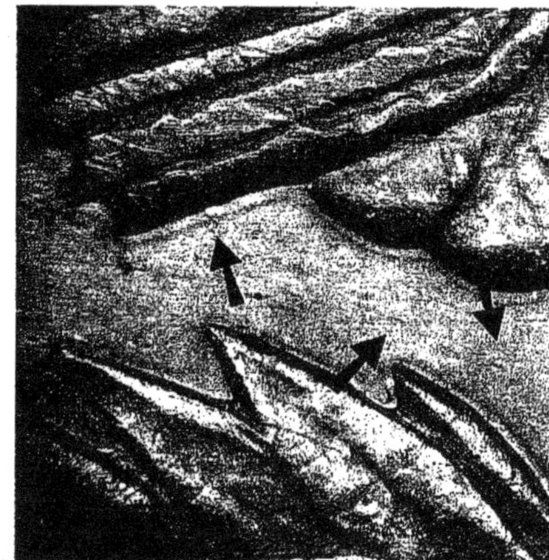
1889 P VAM 1E Four Denticle Impressions

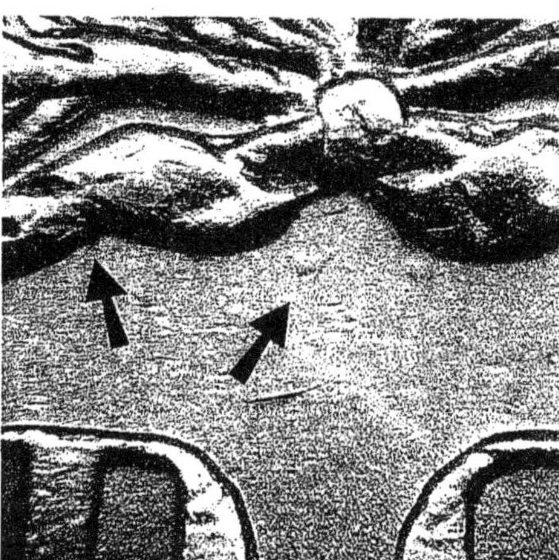
1889 P VAM 1F Denticle Impressions Below Wreath Bow

1889 P VAM 5E Possible Denticle Impression & Die Edge Scratch

1889 P VAM 5E Two Denticle Impressions Bow

1889 P VAM 62 Three Denticle Impressions, Bow With Lines

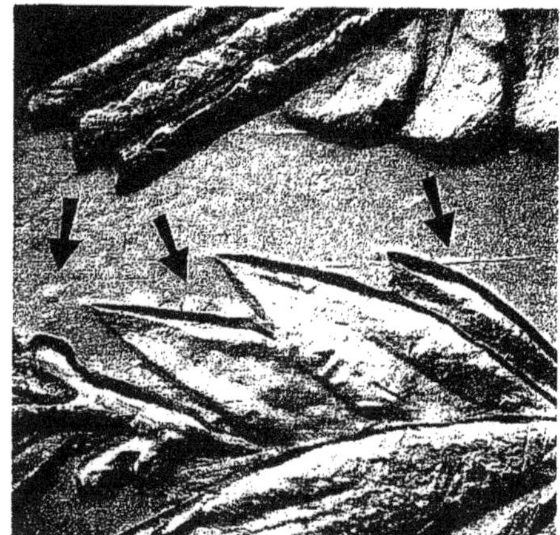
1889 P VAM 14A Denticle & Die Impressions Wreath Leaves

1889 P VAM 14A Denticle Impressions Below TF

1889 P VAM 62 Two Denticle Impressions, Lines Wreath Bow

1889 O VAM 9C Four Denticle Impressions

1889 O VAM 9C Die Scratches Eagle's Right Leg

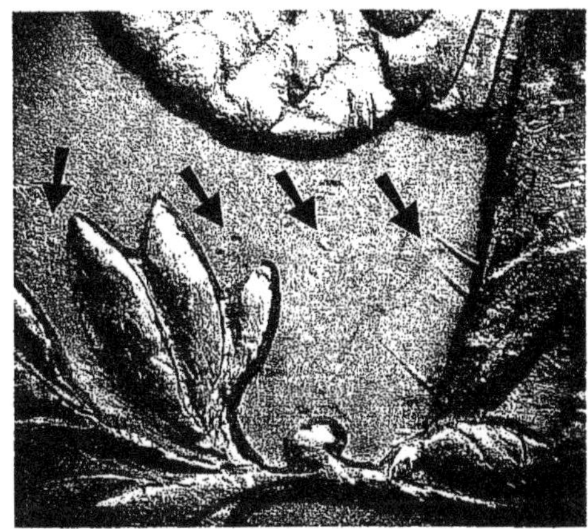
1890 O VAM 1H Denticle & Die Edge Impressions

1890 O VAM 1 I Two Denticle Impressions & Rim Line

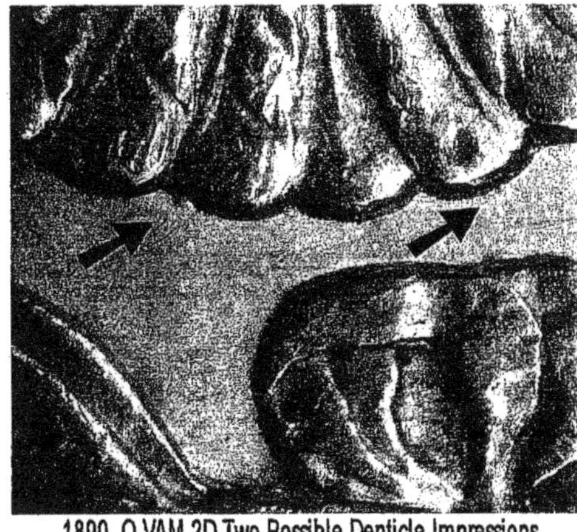
1890 O VAM 2D Two Possible Denticle Impressions

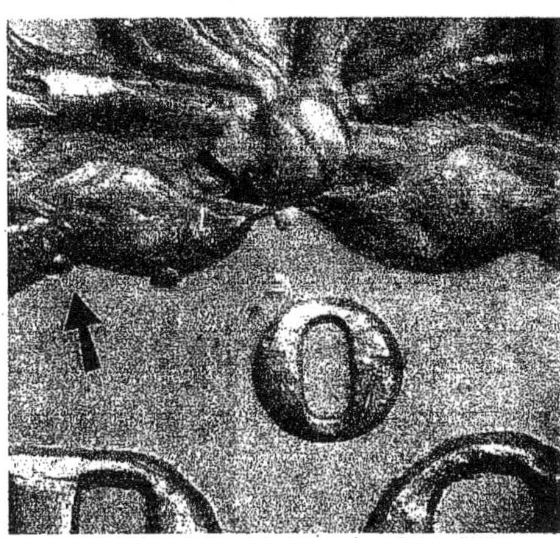
1890 O VAM 16B Denticle Impressions Below Ribbon

1890 O VAM 28B Denticle Impressions Wreath Bow

1891 P VAM 6B Denticle Impressions Eagle's Beak

1900 O VAM 35 Doubled 900, Denticle Impressions

1900 O VAM 47B Three Denticle Impressions

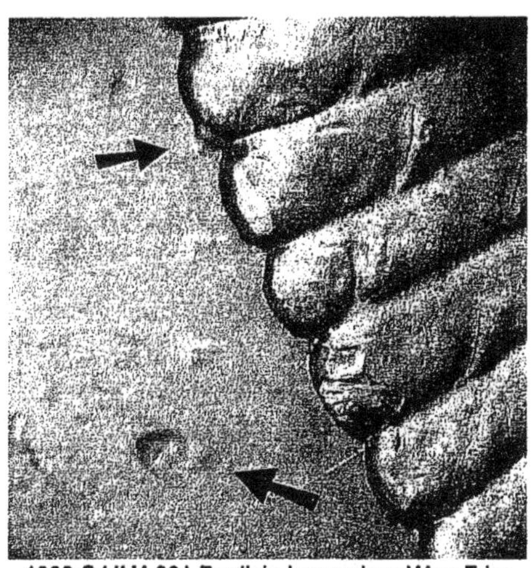
1902 O VAM 90A Denticle Impressions Wing Edge

1921 P VAM 3GM Two Denticle Impressions

GROUPED PHOTOGRAPHS OF PREVIOUSLY LISTED DENTICLE IMPRESSIONS

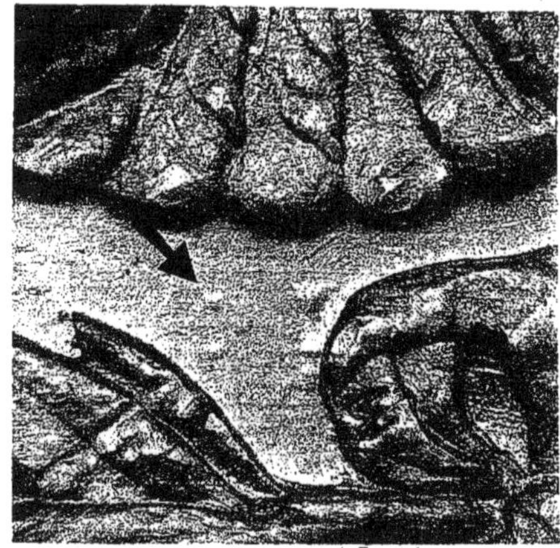

1878 P VAM 221A Denticle Impressions

1878 P VAM 225A Denticle Impressions

1878 CC VAM 20 Denticle Impressions TA

1878 S VAM 17B Denticle Impressions Neck

1878 S VAM 17B Denticle Impressions Date

1878 S VAM 17B Denticle Impressions TF

1878 S VAM 17B Denticle Impressions OLL

1879 P VAM 57A Denticle & Die Edge Impressions

1881 O VAM 18A Denticle & Die Edge Impressions

1883 O VAM 2A Denticle Impressions In

1883 O VAM 2A Denticle Impressions S

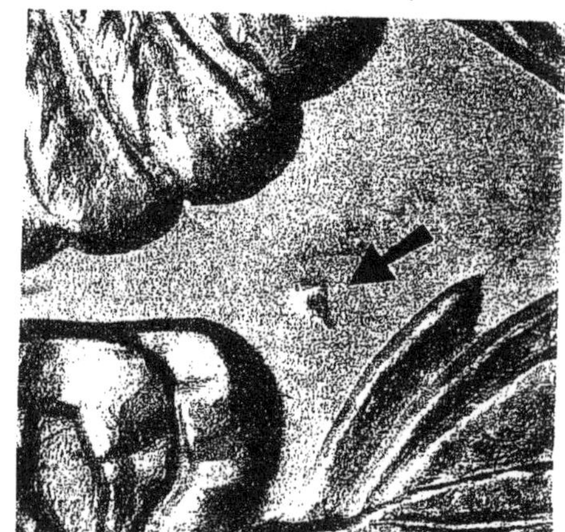

1886 O VAM 1C Raised Triangular Dot

1887 P VAM 1E Denticle Impressions

1888 P VAM 1D Denticle Impressions

1889 P VAM 5D Denticle Impressions
Arrow Feathers

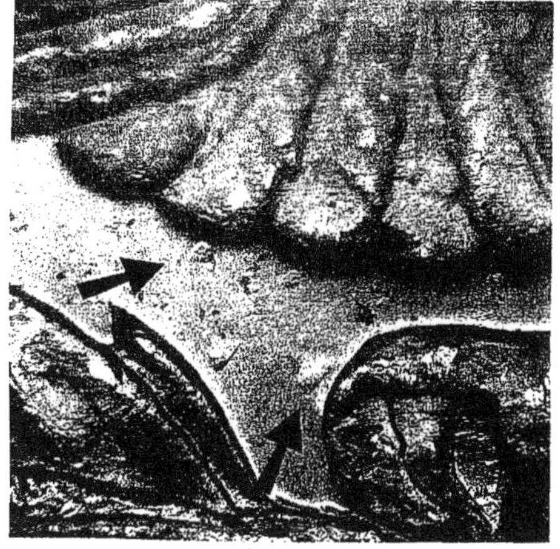
1888 P VAM 17A Denticle Impressions Left

1888 P VAM 17A Denticle Impressions Rt.

1889 P VAM 18B Denticle Impressions
Below Arrow Feathers

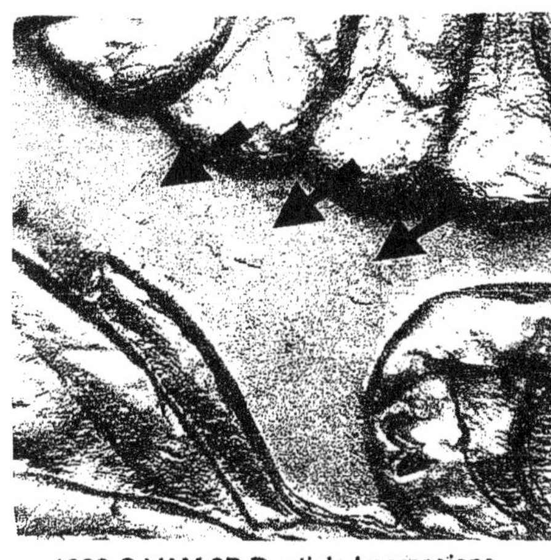
1889 O VAM 9B Denticle Impressions

1889 O VAM 13F Denticle Impressions

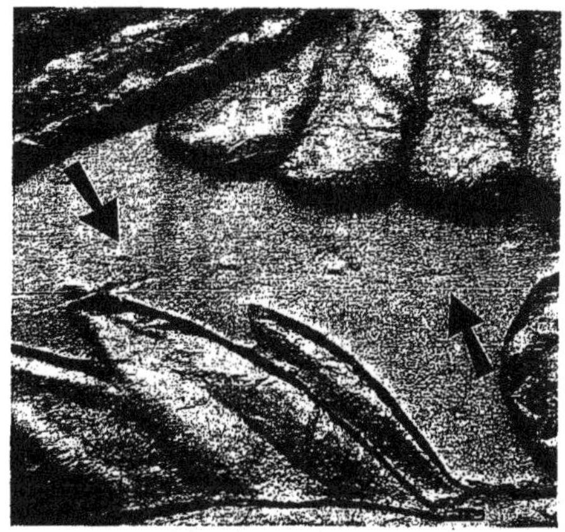
1889 O VAM 16A Denticle Impressions

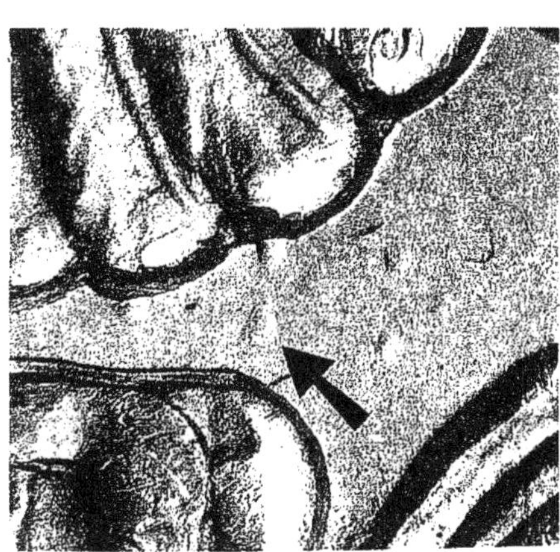
1890 P VAM 1C Denticle Impressions

1890 P VAM 1D Denticle &
Die Edge Impressions

1890 P VAM 1E Denticle Impressions
Below Arrow Feathers

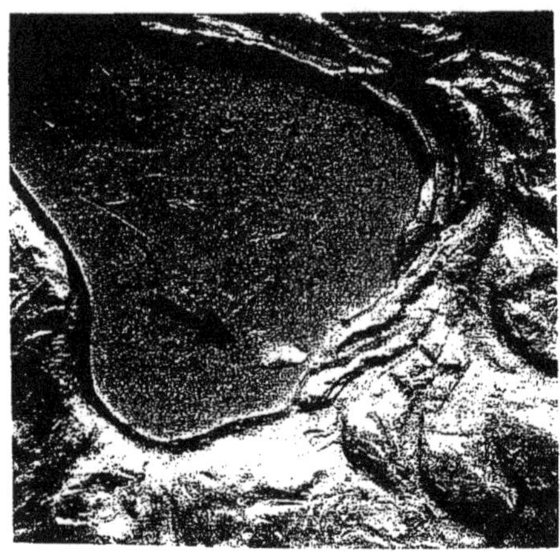

1890 P VAM 1E Denticle Impressions
Eagle's Rt. Shoulder

1890 P VAM 1F Denticle Impressions Rt. Of Leg

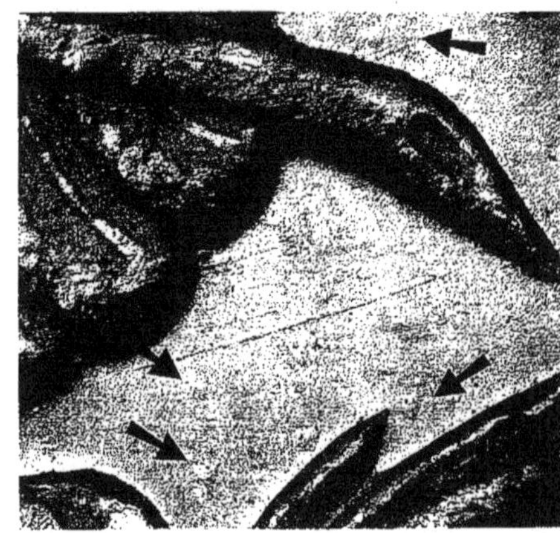

1890 P VAM 1F Denticle Impressions Below TF

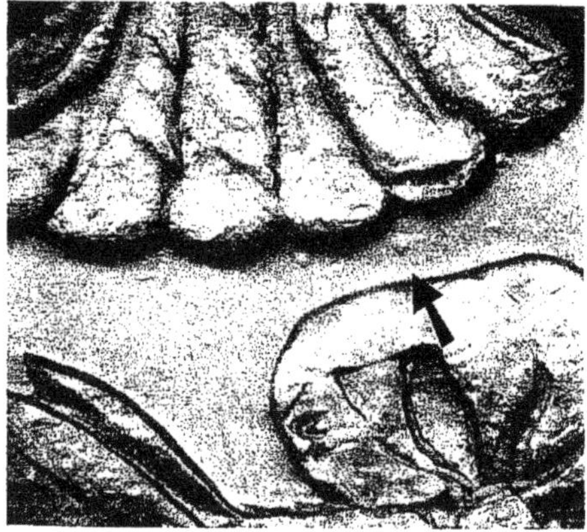

1890 P VAM 1G Denticle Impressions
Middle TF

1890 P VAM 1I Denticle Impressions
Wreath Bow

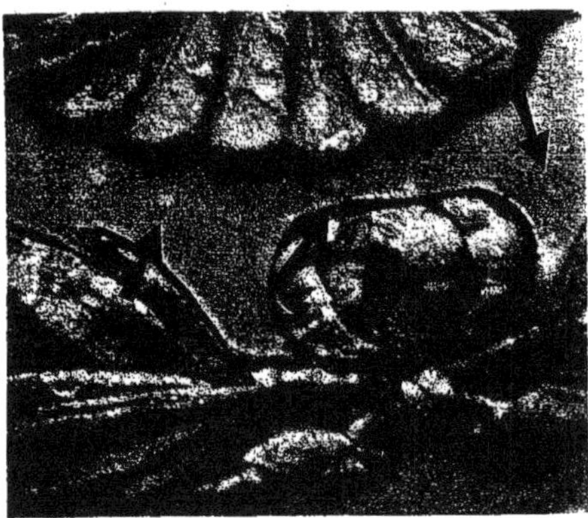

1890 P VAM 4A Denticle Impressions

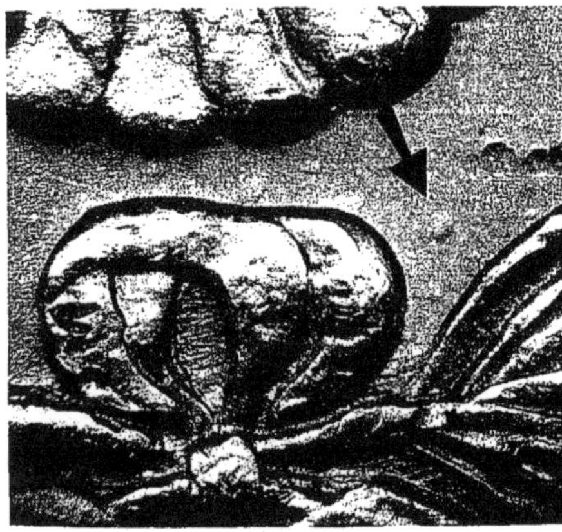

1890 P VAM 11A Denticle Impressions
Wreath Bow

1890 O VAM 1C Denticle Impressions

1890 O VAM 1G Denticle Impressions
Arrow Feathers

1890 O VAM 33A Denticle Impressions
Below Olive Leaves

1890 O VAM 33A Denticle Impressions
Arrow Feathers

1891 P VAM 6A Denticle Impressions
Below TF

1891 P VAM 1B Denticle Impressions

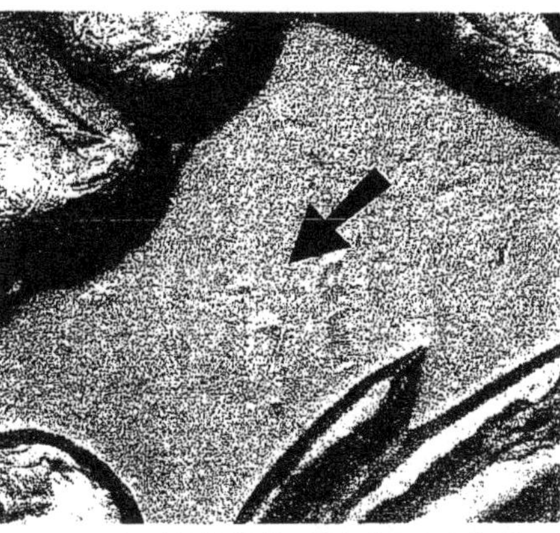

1891 P VAM 1B Denticle Impressions

1891 O VAM 5A Denticle Impressions

1894 O VAM 11B Denticle Impressions, Die Clashes

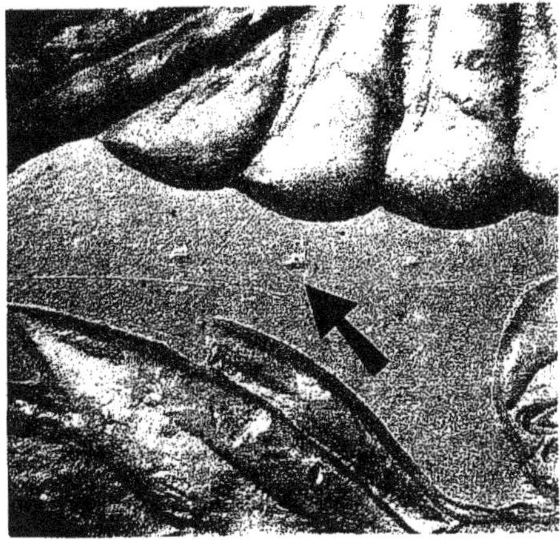

1900 O VAM 21E Denticle Impressions

1901 O VAM 1B Denticle Impression Arrow Feather

1901 O VAM 11A Denticle Impressions Arrow Heads

1901 O VAM 45 2 Denticle Impressions

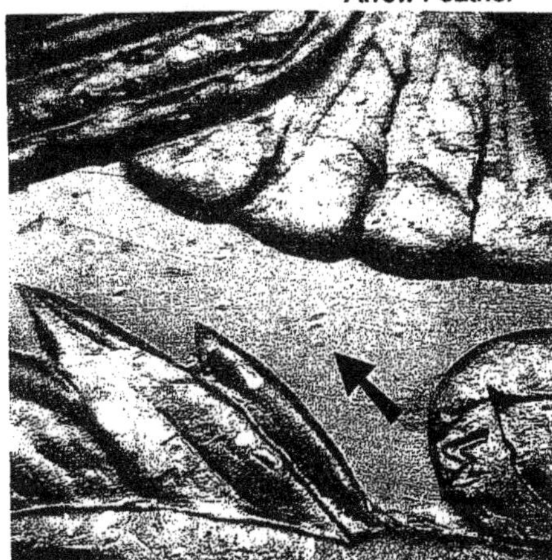

1902 O VAM 44B Denticle Impressions Below TF

1903 P VAM 1B Denticle Impressions Olive Branch

1904 O VAM 30A Denticle Impressions

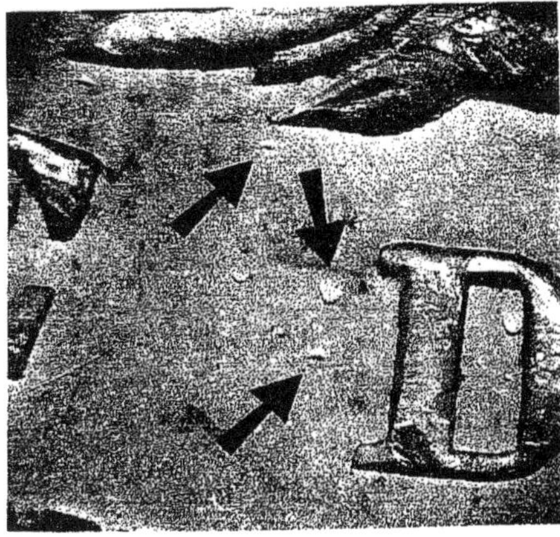

1904 O VAM 30B Denticle Impressions E-D

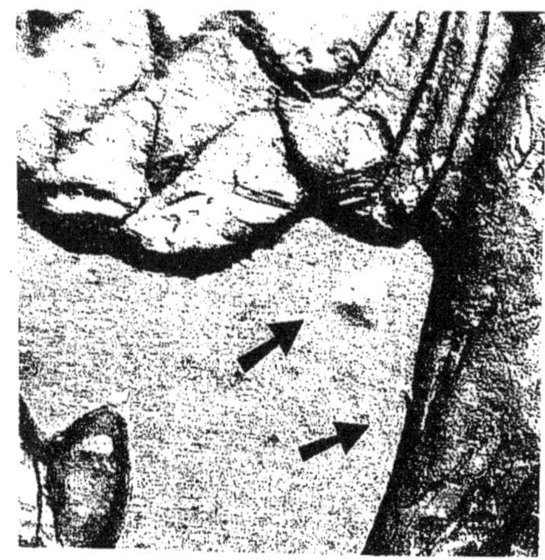
1904 O VAM 22A1 Denticle Impressions
Below Wing

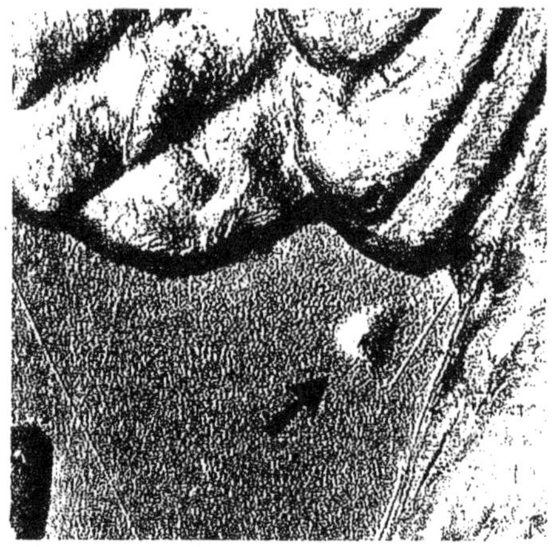
1904 O VAM 12 Denticle Impressions,
Early 2nd Die Combo

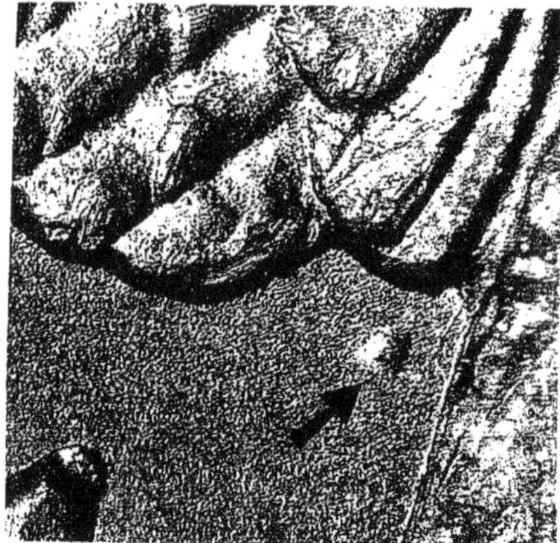
1904 O VAM 12 Denticle Impressions,
Late 2nd Die Combo

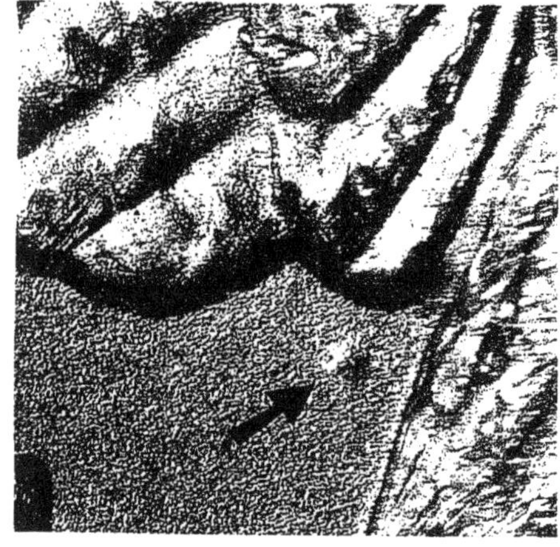
1904 O VAM 22A2 Denticle Impressions,
Late Stage, 3rd Die Combo

1921 P VAM 3F2 Denticle Impressions ME

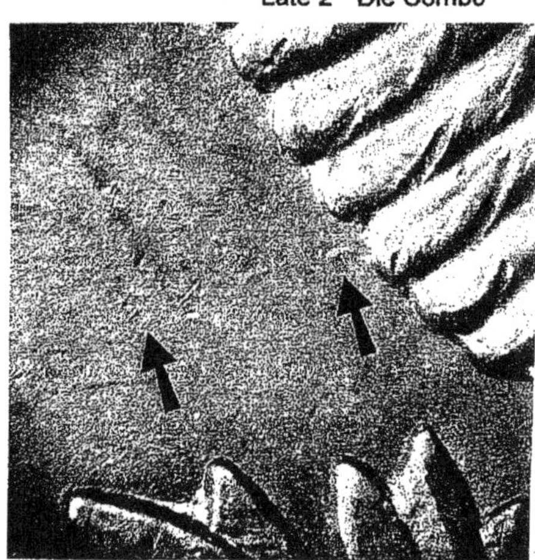
1921 P VAM 3CW2 Denticle Impressions Wing

1921 P VAM 3ER Denticle Impressions IT

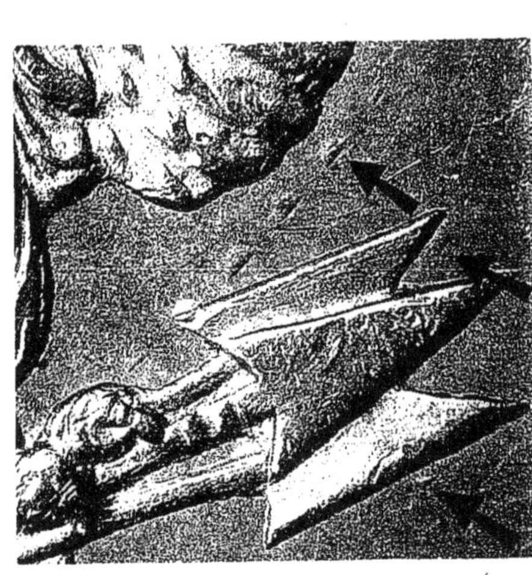
1921 P VAM 31A1 Denticle Impressions

1921 P VAM 31B Two Denticle Impressions

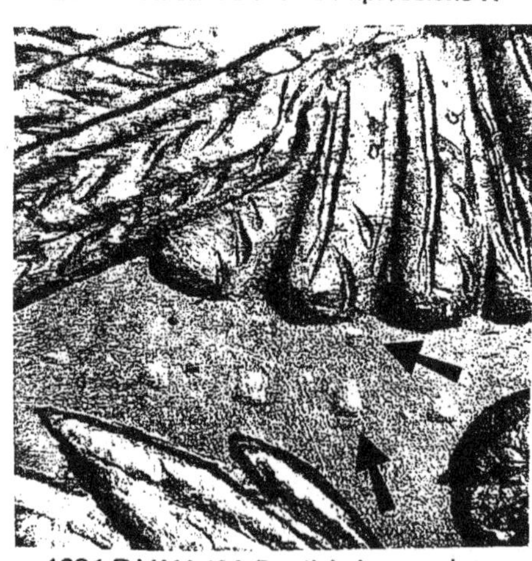
1921 P VAM 40A Denticle Impressions

1921 S VAM 1AJ Two Denticle &
Die Edge Impressions

DENTICLE & DIE EDGE IMPRESSIONS VARIETIES DESCRIPTIVE LISTINGS

1878 P

221-1 II 1 • C^3b (Cut Down A, Doubled Left Reverse, Doubled B) (193) I-2 R-3

Obverse II 1– Die 1– Some specimens show die chip dot on forehead front. Doubled bottom of B in PLURIBUS. Extra metal at top inside of left 8 lower loop and couple polishing lines at eyelid front.

Reverse C^3b– Same hub doubling but different die. Several obverse and reverse dies. Die 1– Vertical polishing line in space to left of eagle's right leg.

221-2 II 1 • C^3b (Cut Down A, Doubled Left Reverse, Polishing Line Cotton Leaf) (193) I-2 R-3

Obverse II 1– Die 2– Diagonal polishing line in hair gap behind neck. Vertical polishing line below right cotton leaf.

Reverse C^3b– Same hub doubling but different die. Several obverse and reverse dies. Die 2– Diagonal polishing lines at top of wing-neck gap.

221A II 1 • C^3b (Cut Down A, Doubled Left Rev., Denticle Impressions Wreath Bow) (180) I-3 R-6

Obverse II 1– Short horizontal die scratch thru middle wheat leaf. (Same die as VAM 227-1.)

Reverse C^3b– Four raised dots in a square to left of wreath bow with lateral spacing of 0.030" of denticle spaces.

225(revised) **II 2 • C^3c (Doubled Lower Reverse) (193) I-2 R-5**

Obverse II 2– Faint short spike or thin diagonal polishing lines below eyelid front on some specimens.

Reverse C^3c– Same hub doubling but different die.

225A II 2 • C^3c (Doubled Lower Reverse, Denticle Impressions on Reverse) (193) I-4 R-5

Obverse II 2– Faint short spike below eyelid front.

Reverse C^3c– Four raised dots below middle tail feathers from impressions of outside of denticles. Spacing between them matches denticle spacing. Short horizontal spikes to right of 1 and 2 tail feathers.

1878 CC

20(revised) **II 1 • B^1g (Medium CC with Dot) (179) I-2 R-5**

Obverse II 1– Line in eye variety, same as VAM 17.

Reverse B^1g– Medium spaced II CC mint mark at medium height. Left C mint mark has die chip in center. Heavy vertical die polishing lines in fields extending from points of letters and design elements.

20A II 1 • B^1g (Medium CC with Dot, Denticle Impressions TA) (179) I-2 R-5

Reverse B^1g– Raised dots of denticle impression between lower serifs of TA in STATES with two faint raised dots between middle of TA and one at top of right inside of lower serif of A. Also shows the field edge line of denticle cavities at TA. Spacing between them matches denticle spacing.

1878 S

17(revised) **II 13 • B^2d (Doubled D, Over Polished Lower Obverse) (184) I-2 R-4**

Obverse II 13– Bottom of die over polished with shallow date and missing portions of lower hair line on later die state. First 8 has small die chip on right side between loops. Part of fourth right star left point completely missing on over polished die state.

Reverse B^2d– D in DOLLAR doubled at left top outside and at left and right bottom outside. Small III S mint mark set slightly to left. R in Trust not broken. Earliest die state has horizontal polishing lines below middle tail feathers. *Die marker–* Die gouge on right ribbon.

17A(revised) **II 13 • B^2d (Doubled D, Denticle Impressions Reverse) (184) I-5 R-6**

Obverse II 13– 7 has raised slanted dash at very bottom. Shallow raised dots at left inside of lower loop of both 8's. Point of fourth right star completely missing. Late die state with most denticle impressions polished and worn away.

Reverse B^2d– Slightly raised denticle impressions band thru O, a band between LL and a double band below OL and four slanted impressions below left tail feathers. Late die state with denticle impressions at UN & STAT weak from die wear.

17B II 13 • B^2d (Doubled D, Denticle Impressions Obverse & Reverse) (184) I-5 R-6

Obverse II 13– Five small raised dots of denticle impressions next to Liberty head neck in field. Six raised dots in band across lower part of date from left inside of left and right 8s and two raised arcs at bottom of 7. Lateral spacing between dots is same as denticle spacing. First reported case of denticle impressions on obverse. VAM 17A doesn't show obverse denticle impressions because of die polishing/wear. VAM 17C doesn't show denticle impressions at date, except for dot inside lower loop of 8 because of die polishing.

Reverse B^2d– Four raised denticle inside end impressions in a band at O, four in band at LL, five in double band below OL and four in slanted band below left tail feathers as in VAM 17A. Four curved raised lines between UN and four above N in UNITED that resemble denticle inside ends. Seven similar curved raised lines above A in STATES and one above right T and five vertical lines above ST with spacing of denticles. Initial denticle impressions die state.

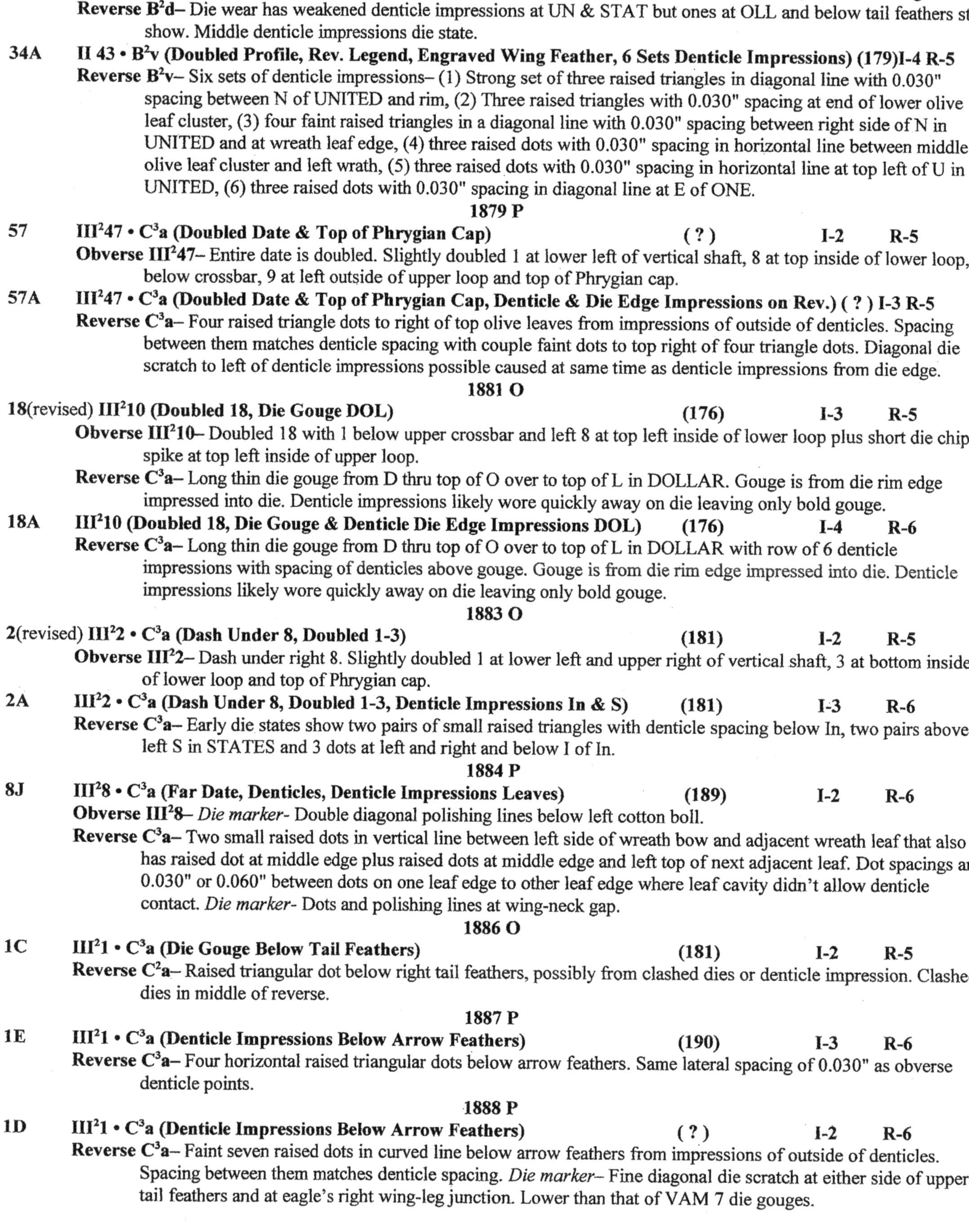

17C **II 13 • B^2d (Doubled D, Denticle Impressions Obverse Neck & Reverse) (184) I-5 R-6**

Obverse II 13– Later die state of VAM 17B with slightly polished die that has removed denticle impressions at date except for one at left inside of both 8s lower loop. Denticle impressions show at Liberty head neck edge.

Reverse B^2d– Die wear has weakened denticle impressions at UN & STAT but ones at OLL and below tail feathers still show. Middle denticle impressions die state.

34A **II 43 • B^2v (Doubled Profile, Rev. Legend, Engraved Wing Feather, 6 Sets Denticle Impressions) (179)I-4 R-5**

Reverse B^2v– Six sets of denticle impressions– (1) Strong set of three raised triangles in diagonal line with 0.030" spacing between N of UNITED and rim, (2) Three raised triangles with 0.030" spacing at end of lower olive leaf cluster, (3) four faint raised triangles in a diagonal line with 0.030" spacing between right side of N in UNITED and at wreath leaf edge, (4) three raised dots with 0.030" spacing in horizontal line between middle olive leaf cluster and left wrath, (5) three raised dots with 0.030" spacing in horizontal line at top left of U in UNITED, (6) three raised dots with 0.030" spacing in diagonal line at E of ONE.

1879 P

57 **$III^2$47 • C^3a (Doubled Date & Top of Phrygian Cap) (?) I-2 R-5**

Obverse $III^2$47– Entire date is doubled. Slightly doubled 1 at lower left of vertical shaft, 8 at top inside of lower loop, 7 below crossbar, 9 at left outside of upper loop and top of Phrygian cap.

57A **$III^2$47 • C^3a (Doubled Date & Top of Phrygian Cap, Denticle & Die Edge Impressions on Rev.) (?) I-3 R-5**

Reverse C^3a– Four raised triangle dots to right of top olive leaves from impressions of outside of denticles. Spacing between them matches denticle spacing with couple faint dots to top right of four triangle dots. Diagonal die scratch to left of denticle impressions possible caused at same time as denticle impressions from die edge.

1881 O

18(revised) **$III^2$10 (Doubled 18, Die Gouge DOL) (176) I-3 R-5**

Obverse $III^2$10– Doubled 18 with 1 below upper crossbar and left 8 at top left inside of lower loop plus short die chip spike at top left inside of upper loop.

Reverse C^3a– Long thin die gouge from D thru top of O over to top of L in DOLLAR. Gouge is from die rim edge impressed into die. Denticle impressions likely wore quickly away on die leaving only bold gouge.

18A **$III^2$10 (Doubled 18, Die Gouge & Denticle Die Edge Impressions DOL) (176) I-4 R-6**

Reverse C^3a– Long thin die gouge from D thru top of O over to top of L in DOLLAR with row of 6 denticle impressions with spacing of denticles above gouge. Gouge is from die rim edge impressed into die. Denticle impressions likely wore quickly away on die leaving only bold gouge.

1883 O

2(revised) **$III^2$2 • C^3a (Dash Under 8, Doubled 1-3) (181) I-2 R-5**

Obverse $III^2$2– Dash under right 8. Slightly doubled 1 at lower left and upper right of vertical shaft, 3 at bottom inside of lower loop and top of Phrygian cap.

2A **$III^2$2 • C^3a (Dash Under 8, Doubled 1-3, Denticle Impressions In & S) (181) I-3 R-6**

Reverse C^3a– Early die states show two pairs of small raised triangles with denticle spacing below In, two pairs above left S in STATES and 3 dots at left and right and below I of In.

1884 P

8J **$III^2$8 • C^3a (Far Date, Denticles, Denticle Impressions Leaves) (189) I-2 R-6**

Obverse $III^2$8– *Die marker-* Double diagonal polishing lines below left cotton boll.

Reverse C^3a– Two small raised dots in vertical line between left side of wreath bow and adjacent wreath leaf that also has raised dot at middle edge plus raised dots at middle edge and left top of next adjacent leaf. Dot spacings are 0.030" or 0.060" between dots on one leaf edge to other leaf edge where leaf cavity didn't allow denticle contact. *Die marker-* Dots and polishing lines at wing-neck gap.

1886 O

1C **$III^2$1 • C^3a (Die Gouge Below Tail Feathers) (181) I-2 R-5**

Reverse C^2a– Raised triangular dot below right tail feathers, possibly from clashed dies or denticle impression. Clashed dies in middle of reverse.

1887 P

1E **$III^2$1 • C^3a (Denticle Impressions Below Arrow Feathers) (190) I-3 R-6**

Reverse C^3a– Four horizontal raised triangular dots below arrow feathers. Same lateral spacing of 0.030" as obverse denticle points.

1888 P

1D **$III^2$1 • C^3a (Denticle Impressions Below Arrow Feathers) (?) I-2 R-6**

Reverse C^3a– Faint seven raised dots in curved line below arrow feathers from impressions of outside of denticles. Spacing between them matches denticle spacing. *Die marker–* Fine diagonal die scratch at either side of upper tail feathers and at eagle's right wing-leg junction. Lower than that of VAM 7 die gouges.

17A III²1 • C³g (Die Chips in 8's, Doubled Reverse, Denticle Impressions Below TF) (189) I-3 R-6
Reverse C³g– Row of 11 shallow small raised dots below tail feathers and around olive branch right end with two large denticle impressions at top left of wreath bow. Same lateral spacing between dots as denticle spacing.

1889 P

1C1(revised) **III²1 • C³a (Die Scratches TF, Denticle Impressions Below TF) (?) I-2 R-6**
Reverse C²a– Two raised triangles below 5 & 6 tail feathers with denticle spacing. Shallow slanted die scratch below middle of tail feathers and short tick below second tail feather from right. Same die as VAM 52 but earlier die state.

1C2(re-instated) **III²1 • C³a (Die Scratches TF) (?) I-2 R-5**
Reverse C²a– Denticle impressions worn away.

1E III²1 • C³a (Denticle Impressions Below Arrow Feathers) (190) I-2 R-6
Obverse III²1– *Die marker*- Long faint vertical polishing line at ear front.
Reverse C³a– Four faint raised dots with denticle spacing below bottom arow feather and 6 & 7 left tail feathers. *Die marker*- Two vertical die scratches below left claw of eagle's left foot.

1F III²1 • C³a (Denticle Impressions Below Wreath Bow) (190) I-2 R-6
Obverse III²1– *Die marker*- Several short vertical polishing lines at top left of ear at hair edge.
Reverse C³a– Two raised dots below wreath bow with denticle spacing of 0.030" plus third smaller dot 0.030" to left at ribbon edge. *Die marker*- Short vertical die scratch at left side of space to left of eagle's right leg.

5D III²5 • C³a (Far Date, Denticle Impressions Below Arrow Feathers) (190) I-2 R-6
Reverse C³a – Partial raised bar at edge of field below bottom arrow feather and small raised triangle at right in field with spacing of denticles. *Die marker*– Die gouge at bottom outside of eagle's right wing.

5E III²5 • C³a (Far Date, Denticle Impressions at Wreath Bow) (190) I-2 R-6
Obverse III²5– *Die marker*– Several horizontal die polishing lines at back of jaw-neck junction.
Reverse C³a– Two raised dots at right of wreath bow with separation spacing of 0.025" that is correct for row separation. Possible third raised dot at top left outside of wreath bow, with possible die edge scratch to left of bow.

14A III²14 • C³a (Doubled 18, Tripled 9, Scribbling on Nose, Denticle Impressions TF & Leaf) (190) I-3 R-6
Reverse C³a– Two rows of faint raised dots below right tail feathers with denticle spacings. Three raised dots at edge of upper left leaf of fist left wreath leaf cluster with denticle spacing. Possible die edge curved raised line impression at top of first left leaf cluster.

18(revised) **III²18 • C³a (Doubled Ear, Slanted Very Far Date) (190) I-3 R-4**
Obverse III²18– Ear slightly doubled at left inside and right outside. Slightly doubled lower edge of hair above ear and lower cotton leaves. Slanted date set much further right than normal with 1 higher than 9. *Diagnostic*– Slanted very far date with 1 higher than 9.

18A III²18 • C³a (Doubled Ear, Slanted Very Far Date, Die Chip Cap Rear) (190) I-3 R-6
Obverse III²18– Small die chip at back of Phrygian cap near right tip of upper leaf of lower cotton of lower cotton leaf cluster.

18B III²18 • C³a (Doubled Ear, Slanted Very Far Date, Denticle Impressions Below Arrow Feathers) (190)I-3 R-6
Reverse C³a– Three raised triangles in a row with denticle spacing below arrow feathers. Occurred before VAM 18A on initial die state but likely disappeared quickly from die wear.

62 III²57 • C³a (Far Date, High 9, Denticle Impressions Wreath Bow) (190) I-2 R-6
Obverse III²57– Date set further right than normal with high 9. *Die marker*- Diagonal die scratch back of Liberty head neck near hair.
Reverse C³a– Three triangle raised dots at left side of wreath bow and two at upper right side of wreath bow with denticle spacing of 0.030". Also has three denticle impression triangles at first left wreath berry cluster with spacing of 0.030". *Die marker*- Polishing lines in wreath bow.

1889 O

9B III²1 • C³f (O Set High, Denticle Impressions on Reverse) (181) I-3 R-6
Reverse C²f– Three raised dots below left tail feathers from impressions of outside of denticles. Spacing between them matches denticle spacing. II O mint mark set upright and high.

9C III²1 • C³f (O Set High, Denticle Impressions Arrow Shaft) (181) I-2 R-6
Obverse III²1– Triangle inner & outer denticle spaces.
Reverse C³f– Four raised triangles at arrow feather ends over to lower olive leaves with strong triangle at arrow feather end with spacing of 0.030" of obverse denticles. Slightly curved die scratch below left tail feather end possible from obverse die rim edge. III O mint mark set upright and high. *Die marker*- Horizontal polishing line across middle tail feathers. Some short horizontal die scratches at left outside of eagle's right leg.

13F **III^{2}8 • C^{3}a (Far Date, Denticle Impressions Below Arrow Feathers) (181) I-2 R-6**

Reverse C^{3}a– Faint impressions of outside of denticles in three rows below arrow feathers. Top row has four dots to left and right of lower arrow father. Middle row has four dots below arrow feathers. Lower row has single dot above wreath top berry.

16A **III^{2}8 • C^{3}f (Far Date, High O, Denticle Impressions Below Tail Feathers) (181) I-2 R-6**

Reverse C^{3}f– Four raised dots below left tail feathers from impressions of outside of denticles with spacing between them that matches denticle spacing. III O mint mark set upright and high. Denticle impressions higher than VAM 9B.

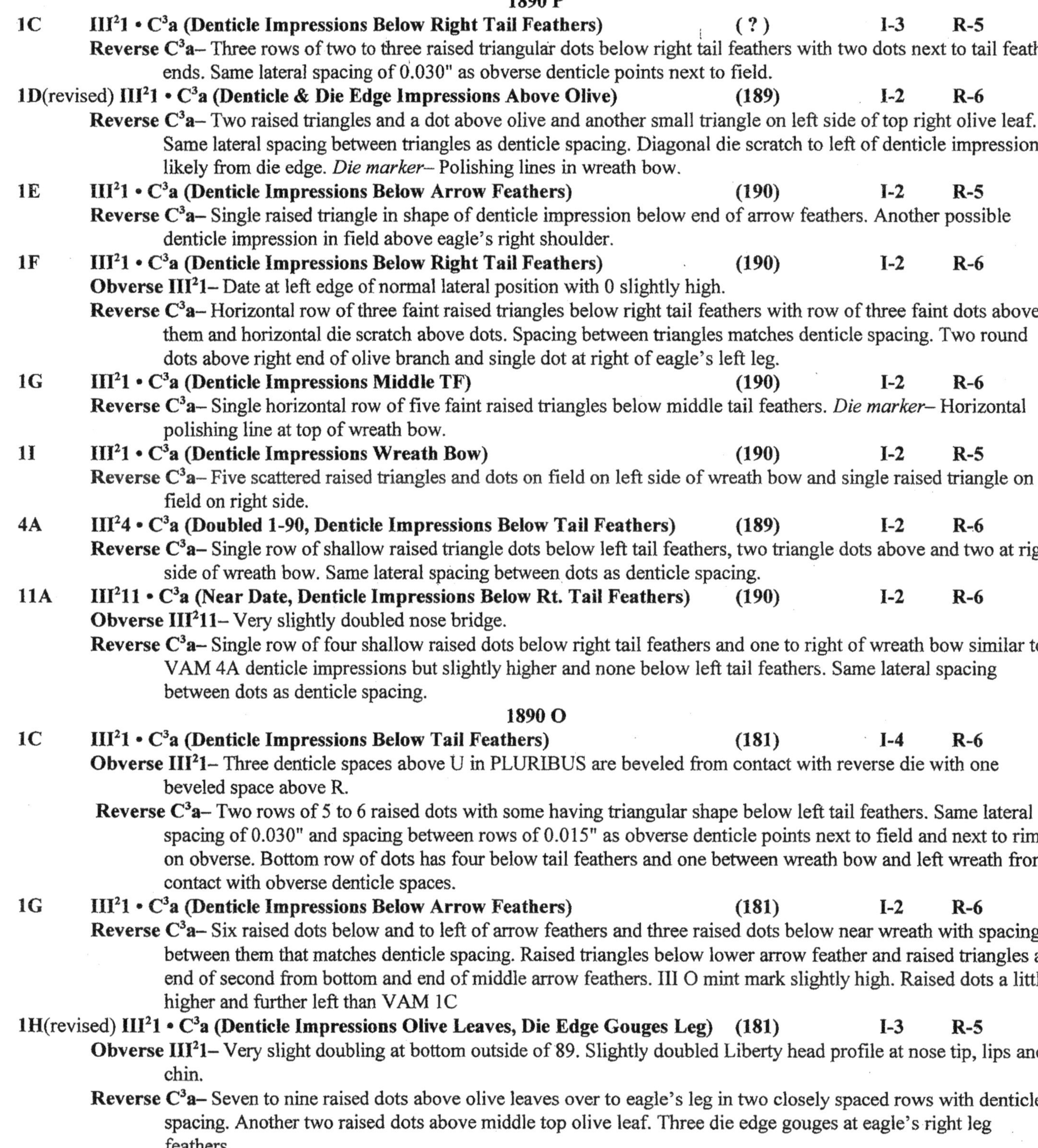

1890 P

1C **III^{2}1 • C^{3}a (Denticle Impressions Below Right Tail Feathers) (?) I-3 R-5**

Reverse C^{3}a– Three rows of two to three raised triangular dots below right tail feathers with two dots next to tail feather ends. Same lateral spacing of 0.030" as obverse denticle points next to field.

1D(revised) **III^{2}1 • C^{3}a (Denticle & Die Edge Impressions Above Olive) (189) I-2 R-6**

Reverse C^{3}a– Two raised triangles and a dot above olive and another small triangle on left side of top right olive leaf. Same lateral spacing between triangles as denticle spacing. Diagonal die scratch to left of denticle impressions likely from die edge. *Die marker–* Polishing lines in wreath bow.

1E **III^{2}1 • C^{3}a (Denticle Impressions Below Arrow Feathers) (190) I-2 R-5**

Reverse C^{3}a– Single raised triangle in shape of denticle impression below end of arrow feathers. Another possible denticle impression in field above eagle's right shoulder.

1F **III^{2}1 • C^{3}a (Denticle Impressions Below Right Tail Feathers) (190) I-2 R-6**

Obverse III^{2}1– Date at left edge of normal lateral position with 0 slightly high.

Reverse C^{3}a– Horizontal row of three faint raised triangles below right tail feathers with row of three faint dots above them and horizontal die scratch above dots. Spacing between triangles matches denticle spacing. Two round dots above right end of olive branch and single dot at right of eagle's left leg.

1G **III^{2}1 • C^{3}a (Denticle Impressions Middle TF) (190) I-2 R-6**

Reverse C^{3}a– Single horizontal row of five faint raised triangles below middle tail feathers. *Die marker–* Horizontal polishing line at top of wreath bow.

1I **III^{2}1 • C^{3}a (Denticle Impressions Wreath Bow) (190) I-2 R-5**

Reverse C^{3}a– Five scattered raised triangles and dots on field on left side of wreath bow and single raised triangle on field on right side.

4A **III^{2}4 • C^{3}a (Doubled 1-90, Denticle Impressions Below Tail Feathers) (189) I-2 R-6**

Reverse C^{3}a– Single row of shallow raised triangle dots below left tail feathers, two triangle dots above and two at right side of wreath bow. Same lateral spacing between dots as denticle spacing.

11A **III^{2}11 • C^{3}a (Near Date, Denticle Impressions Below Rt. Tail Feathers) (190) I-2 R-6**

Obverse III^{2}11– Very slightly doubled nose bridge.

Reverse C^{3}a– Single row of four shallow raised dots below right tail feathers and one to right of wreath bow similar to VAM 4A denticle impressions but slightly higher and none below left tail feathers. Same lateral spacing between dots as denticle spacing.

1890 O

1C **III^{2}1 • C^{3}a (Denticle Impressions Below Tail Feathers) (181) I-4 R-6**

Obverse III^{2}1– Three denticle spaces above U in PLURIBUS are beveled from contact with reverse die with one beveled space above R.

Reverse C^{3}a– Two rows of 5 to 6 raised dots with some having triangular shape below left tail feathers. Same lateral spacing of 0.030" and spacing between rows of 0.015" as obverse denticle points next to field and next to rim on obverse. Bottom row of dots has four below tail feathers and one between wreath bow and left wreath from contact with obverse denticle spaces.

1G **III^{2}1 • C^{3}a (Denticle Impressions Below Arrow Feathers) (181) I-2 R-6**

Reverse C^{3}a– Six raised dots below and to left of arrow feathers and three raised dots below near wreath with spacing between them that matches denticle spacing. Raised triangles below lower arrow feather and raised triangles at end of second from bottom and end of middle arrow feathers. III O mint mark slightly high. Raised dots a little higher and further left than VAM 1C

1H(revised) **III^{2}1 • C^{3}a (Denticle Impressions Olive Leaves, Die Edge Gouges Leg) (181) I-3 R-5**

Obverse III^{2}1– Very slight doubling at bottom outside of 89. Slightly doubled Liberty head profile at nose tip, lips and chin.

Reverse C^{3}a– Seven to nine raised dots above olive leaves over to eagle's leg in two closely spaced rows with denticle spacing. Another two raised dots above middle top olive leaf. Three die edge gouges at eagle's right leg feathers.

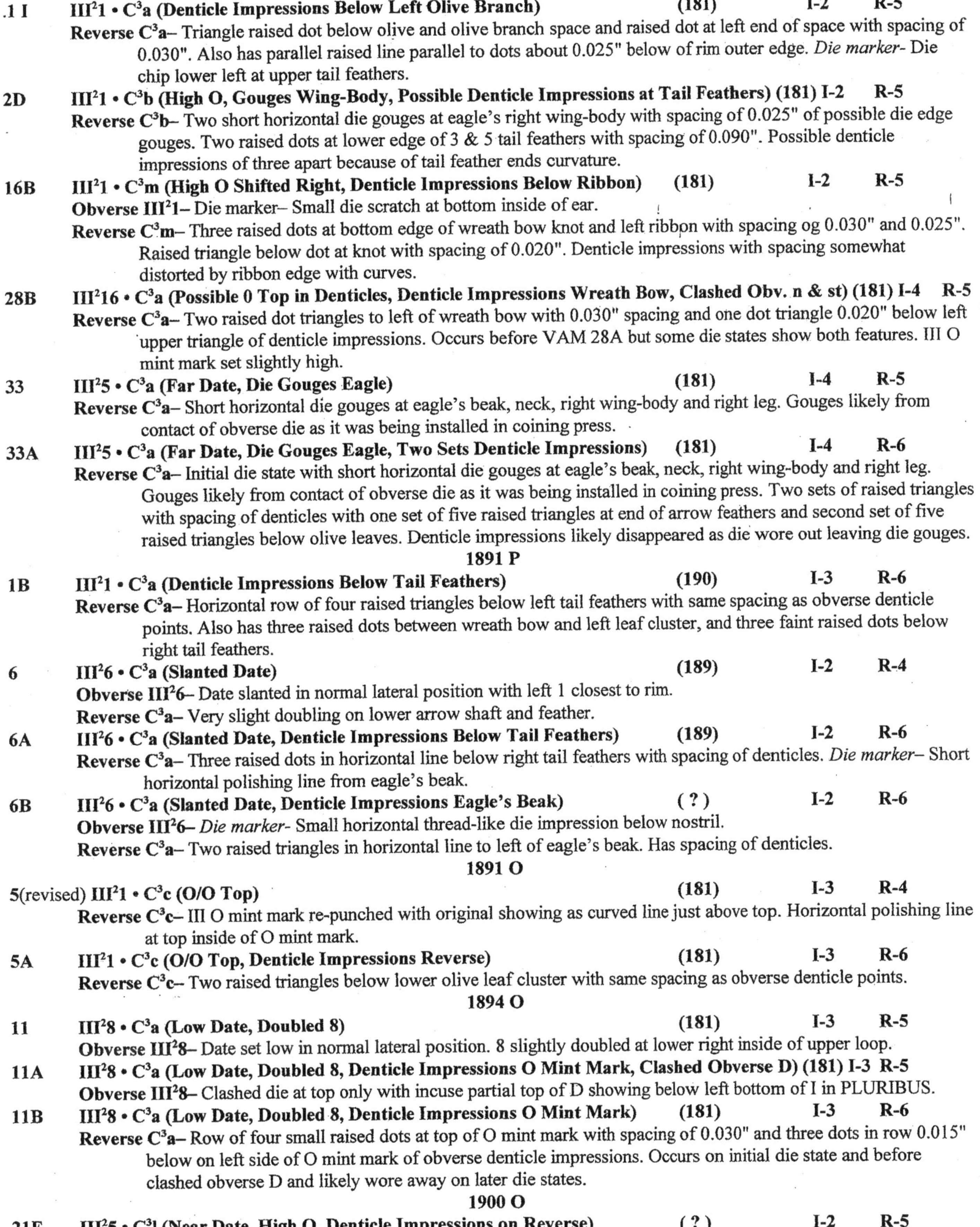

11 **III^{2}1 • C^{3}a (Denticle Impressions Below Left Olive Branch) (181) I-2 R-5**
Reverse C^{3}a– Triangle raised dot below olive and olive branch space and raised dot at left end of space with spacing of 0.030". Also has parallel raised line parallel to dots about 0.025" below of rim outer edge. *Die marker-* Die chip lower left at upper tail feathers.

2D **III^{2}1 • C^{3}b (High O, Gouges Wing-Body, Possible Denticle Impressions at Tail Feathers) (181) I-2 R-5**
Reverse C^{3}b– Two short horizontal die gouges at eagle's right wing-body with spacing of 0.025" of possible die edge gouges. Two raised dots at lower edge of 3 & 5 tail feathers with spacing of 0.090". Possible denticle impressions of three apart because of tail feather ends curvature.

16B **III^{2}1 • C^{3}m (High O Shifted Right, Denticle Impressions Below Ribbon) (181) I-2 R-5**
Obverse III^{2}1– Die marker– Small die scratch at bottom inside of ear.
Reverse C^{3}m– Three raised dots at bottom edge of wreath bow knot and left ribbon with spacing og 0.030" and 0.025". Raised triangle below dot at knot with spacing of 0.020". Denticle impressions with spacing somewhat distorted by ribbon edge with curves.

28B **III^{2}16 • C^{3}a (Possible 0 Top in Denticles, Denticle Impressions Wreath Bow, Clashed Obv. n & st) (181) I-4 R-5**
Reverse C^{3}a– Two raised dot triangles to left of wreath bow with 0.030" spacing and one dot triangle 0.020" below left upper triangle of denticle impressions. Occurs before VAM 28A but some die states show both features. III O mint mark set slightly high.

33 **III^{2}5 • C^{3}a (Far Date, Die Gouges Eagle) (181) I-4 R-5**
Reverse C^{3}a– Short horizontal die gouges at eagle's beak, neck, right wing-body and right leg. Gouges likely from contact of obverse die as it was being installed in coining press.

33A **III^{2}5 • C^{3}a (Far Date, Die Gouges Eagle, Two Sets Denticle Impressions) (181) I-4 R-6**
Reverse C^{3}a– Initial die state with short horizontal die gouges at eagle's beak, neck, right wing-body and right leg. Gouges likely from contact of obverse die as it was being installed in coining press. Two sets of raised triangles with spacing of denticles with one set of five raised triangles at end of arrow feathers and second set of five raised triangles below olive leaves. Denticle impressions likely disappeared as die wore out leaving die gouges.

1891 P

1B **III^{2}1 • C^{3}a (Denticle Impressions Below Tail Feathers) (190) I-3 R-6**
Reverse C^{3}a– Horizontal row of four raised triangles below left tail feathers with same spacing as obverse denticle points. Also has three raised dots between wreath bow and left leaf cluster, and three faint raised dots below right tail feathers.

6 **III^{2}6 • C^{3}a (Slanted Date) (189) I-2 R-4**
Obverse III^{2}6– Date slanted in normal lateral position with left 1 closest to rim.
Reverse C^{3}a– Very slight doubling on lower arrow shaft and feather.

6A **III^{2}6 • C^{3}a (Slanted Date, Denticle Impressions Below Tail Feathers) (189) I-2 R-6**
Reverse C^{3}a– Three raised dots in horizontal line below right tail feathers with spacing of denticles. *Die marker–* Short horizontal polishing line from eagle's beak.

6B **III^{2}6 • C^{3}a (Slanted Date, Denticle Impressions Eagle's Beak) (?) I-2 R-6**
Obverse III^{2}6– *Die marker-* Small horizontal thread-like die impression below nostril.
Reverse C^{3}a– Two raised triangles in horizontal line to left of eagle's beak. Has spacing of denticles.

1891 O

5(revised) **III^{2}1 • C^{3}c (O/O Top) (181) I-3 R-4**
Reverse C^{3}c– III O mint mark re-punched with original showing as curved line just above top. Horizontal polishing line at top inside of O mint mark.

5A **III^{2}1 • C^{3}c (O/O Top, Denticle Impressions Reverse) (181) I-3 R-6**
Reverse C^{3}c– Two raised triangles below lower olive leaf cluster with same spacing as obverse denticle points.

1894 O

11 **III^{2}8 • C^{3}a (Low Date, Doubled 8) (181) I-3 R-5**
Obverse III^{2}8– Date set low in normal lateral position. 8 slightly doubled at lower right inside of upper loop.

11A **III^{2}8 • C^{3}a (Low Date, Doubled 8, Denticle Impressions O Mint Mark, Clashed Obverse D) (181) I-3 R-5**
Obverse III^{2}8– Clashed die at top only with incuse partial top of D showing below left bottom of I in PLURIBUS.

11B **III^{2}8 • C^{3}a (Low Date, Doubled 8, Denticle Impressions O Mint Mark) (181) I-3 R-6**
Reverse C^{3}a– Row of four small raised dots at top of O mint mark with spacing of 0.030" and three dots in row 0.015" below on left side of O mint mark of obverse denticle impressions. Occurs on initial die state and before clashed obverse D and likely wore away on later die states.

1900 O

21E **III^{2}5 • C^{3}l (Near Date, High O, Denticle Impressions on Reverse) (?) I-2 R-5**
Obverse III^{2}5– *Die marker–* Heavy diagonal polishing line below ear.

Reverse C³l– Three small raised dots below left tail feathers from impressions of outside of denticles. Spacing between them matches denticle spacing.

35(re-instated) **III²22 • C³l (Doubled 900 & Ear, High O, Near Date, Possible Denticle Impressions) (?) I-2 R-5**

Obverse III²22– Doubled 900 with 900 at top inside and right 0 also at top outside. Ear doubled at right inside. Date set further left than normal. *Die marker*– Two raised dots at hair edge above 00 of date with 0.030" spacing of ***possible*** denticle impressions. Die cracks at bottom of date match VAM book photo of VAM 35. Doubling at top inside of right 0 and strongly doubled ear different than VAM 14.

Reverse C³l– *Die marker*– Short diagonal polishing line on second inner feather from bottom of eagle's left wing.

35A III²22 • C³l (Doubled 900 & Ear, High O, Near Date, Clashed Obverse n) (?) I-2 R-5

Obverse III²22– Clashed die with partial incuse n of In from reverse showing next to Liberty head neck. Die cracks at date digit bottoms with slight displaced field breaks on later die states.

47B(revised) **III²5 • C³a (Near Date, Die Gouges Wing, Denticle Impressions D) (187) I-3 R-5**

Obverse III²5– Near date. Raised dots on 900 digits on lower part of vertical stems.

Reverse C³a– Slightly double/tripled UNITED letter bottoms towards rim;. Couple left wreath leaves doubled. Three short diagonal die gouges at junction of eagle's left wing and leg. Series of vertical die scratches in eagle's left wing at junction of inner and outer feathers. Vertical die gouge at top of eagle's left wing. Couple short vertical die scratches in top of eagle's right wing.

Three raised triangular denticle impressions with one in lower middle of D of DOLLAR, small raised triangle at 0.030" to left outside edge of D and faint raised triangle between D and O 0.060' from one inside D. (0.030" to right of one inside D is at right leg of D die cavity and therefore couldn't make die impression there.)

1901 O

1B III²1 • C³a (Die Scratches Eagle's Neck, Denticle Impressions Above Arrow Feathers) (181) I-2 R-6

Reverse C³a– Several long vertical die scratches at neck and above eagle's right shoulder. Single small denticle impression above arrow feathers.

11(revised) **III²6 • C⁴b (Slanted Date, O Tilted Left) (181) I-3 R-5**

Obverse III²6– Die 1– Date slanted and in normal lateral position with 1 higher than left 1. *Die marker*– Horizontal die scratch below eye. Die 2– Date slanted and in normal lateral position with right 1 higher than left 1. Faint thin curved thread-like die impression below lowest cotton leaf.

Reverse C⁴b– Die 1-- Slight doubling/tripling of bottom inside of legend letters of C⁴ hub doubling. Die 2– Two vertical rows of four raised dots each to right of lower arrow head from impression of denticles. Spacing between them matches denticle spacing. Slight hub doubling of UNITED STATES OF AMERICA towards rim. *Die marker*– Two thin diagonal die scratches at left wreath outside opposite N in UNITED.

11A III²6 • C⁴b (Slanted Date, O Tilted Left, Denticle Impressions Reverse) (181) I-3 R-6

Reverse C⁴b– Die 2– Two vertical rows of four raised dots each to right of lower arrow head from impression of denticles. Spacing between them matches denticle spacing.

45 III²1 • C⁴/C³t (2 Olive Rev. Die Gouges Leg, Denticle Impressions Shoulder) (181) I-3 R-6

Reverse C⁴/C³t– Extra olive to right of olive connected to olive branch. Doubling at lower edge of middle and lower olive leaves, bottom of lower arrow feathers back of lower arrow head, feathers at top of eagle's left wing and right side of eagle's nostril. III O mint mark centered with slight tilt to left. Two short horizontal die gouges on left side of eagle's right leg. Two strong raised triangles at edge of eagle's right shoulder with same spacing as obverse denticle points.

1902 O

44B III²15 • C⁴n (Doubled Profile, Rev. Lettering, Near Date, Denticle Impressions Below TF) (181) I-2 R-6

Obverse III²15– No die scratches on upper lip.

Reverse C⁴n– Four faint tiny raised dots below left tail feathers from impression of outside of denticles. Spacing between them matches denticle spacing. Only visible on early die state specimens.

90 III²28 • C⁴v (Doubled Profile & Reverse Lettering, Near Date, High O, 2 In Denticles) (181) I-3 R-5

Obverse III²28– Date at right side of near date lateral position. Top of 2 showing in denticles as raised curved bars in two adjacent denticle spaces below 02. Doubled nose, lips and chin on Liberty head profile. *Die marker*– Long vertical die scratch in hair back of Neck.

Reverse C⁴v– Hub doubled lettering as on VAM 26 C⁴l. O mint mark set high, slightly right and tilted slightly left. *Die marker*– A few raised die rust pits between AR in DOLLAR and third outer feather from bottom of eagle's right wing.

90A III²28 • C⁴v (Doubled Profile & Rev. Lettering, Near Date, High O, 2 In Denticles, Denticle Impression Wing) (181) I-3 R-6

Reverse C⁴v– Four raised dots in vertical line from ninth outer feather from bottom of eagle's right wing. Spacing between them matches denticle spacing.

1903 P

1B **III²1 • C⁴a (Denticle Impressions Below Olive Branch End)** (189) I-3 R-6

Reverse C⁴a– Three rows of denticle impressions of outside of denticles with three small raised triangles at olive branch end tip, four raised triangles below tip and two raised triangles between wreath leaves. Spacing between triangles matches denticle spacings.

1904 O

12(revised) **III²8 • C⁴b (Doubled 9-4, O Tilted Left, Denticle Impressions Below Wing, Overlapping Reeding)** (189) I-2 R-4

Obverse III²8– Doubled 9-4 in date. Doubled 9 at bottom outside of both loops. 4 slightly doubled on left side of lower half of vertical shaft on fully struck specimens. Doubled profile from front of LIBERTY band down to neck and hair edge above date. Very slightly doubled some left stars and PLUR towards rim. *Die marker*– Short horizontal die scratch at eye front.

Reverse C⁴b– Has faint polished remnant of raised triangle below bottom inner feather of eagle's right wing of VAM 22A. No die gouge in O of ONE.

Edge– Overlapping reeding of about 14 segments at 3:30 and 6 segments at 11 or 10:30 & 6 o'clock.

22A1(revised) **III²7 • C⁴b (Doubled Profile, O Tilted Left, Denticle Impressions Below Wing) (181)** I-3 R-6

Obverse III²7– Die 1 has doubled profile from hair down to chin with date on left side of normal position. Used with earliest reverse die state of denticle impression below wing.

Reverse C⁴b– Raised triangle below bottom inner feather of eagle's right wing. Shape matches that of some other listed denticle impressions varieties. Also has short raised line on edge of eagle's right leg. Earliest die state with obverse die 1.

22A2(revised) **III²7 • C⁴b (Dbld Profile, O Tilted Left, Denticle Impressions Wing, Overlapping Reeding) (?) I-3 R-6**

Obverse III²7– Die 2 has slightly doubled profile from hair down to chin with date on right side of normal position and diagonal polishing lines thru TY. Used with latest reverse die state of denticle impressions below wing after VAM 12 die combo.

Reverse C⁴b– Latest die state of denticle impression with obverse die 2 after VAM 12 combo with added faint die gouge above O in ONE and faint polished down denticle impression.

Edge– Reeding is overlapping for about 14 segments at 12 o'clock and about 6 segments at 7:30 o'clock and also 2:30 & 10 or 6:30 & 2.

30A **III²7 • C⁴h (Doubled Profile, High O Tilted Left, Denticle Impressions Arrow Head) (181)** I-3 R-6

Reverse C⁴h– Two raised triangles below lower arrow head with 0.030" spacing that matches denticle spacing. Third raised triangle at top edge of middle arrow head. Faint dots at left of each triangle from inner part of denticles.

30B **III²7 • C⁴h (Doubled Profile, High O Tilted Left, Denticle Impressions E-D) (?)** I-3 R-6

Reverse C⁴h– Raised triangle inside D of DOLLAR, Two at left side of D and small triangle below middle one. Three faint small raised dots above right side of E in ONE. Several short die scratches at top edge of eagle's right wing.

1921 P

3F1(revised) **IV 1 • D²a (Die Gouge Wing, Scribbling Die Scratches #43)** (189) I-3 R-5

Obverse IV 1– Two different dies used, one with faintly double nose profile.

Reverse D²a– Heavy horizontal die gouge thru bottom of eagle's right wing. (Formerly VAM 1K.) Fine die scratches in various directions on over polished tail feathers around eagle's right leg, between eagle's left wing and body and in middle of both wings.

3F2 **IV 1 • D²a (Die Gouge Wing, Denticle Impressions ME)** (189) I-3 R-6

Reverse D²a– Four denticle impressions raised dots with faint left fifth dot in horizontal line and possible two round dots below line between ME in AMERICA over to top of wreath from impressions of outside of die denticles. Spacing between dots matches denticle spacings of 0.030".

3F3 **IV 1 • D²a (Die Gouge Wing, Pitted Reverse, Denticle Impressions ME)** (189) I-3 R-6

Reverse D²a– Raised dots from rust pitted die around lower right wreath, AR in DOLLAR, above first S in STATES and below first A in AMERICA. Also has gouge in wing.

3F4 **IV 1 • D²a (Die Gouge Wing, Pitted Reverse, Die Break Above R)** (189) I-3 R-7

Reverse D²a– Radial die crack left side of R in AMERICA with diagonal die crack from top left of R over to denticles where it becomes a break. Denticle impressions at ME no longer visible from die wear.

3CW2 **IV 1 • D²a (Scribbles Cheek, Leg & Wing, Denticle Impressions Wing)** (189) I-4 R-6

Reverse D²a– Four faint denticle impressions raised dots in a horizontal line opposite fourth outer feather from bottom of eagle's right wing. Spacing between dots matches denticle spacings.

3ER IV 1 • D^2a (Scribbling Die Scratches #105 & on Cheek, Denticle Impressions IT) (189) I-3 R-5

Obverse IV 1– Scribbling die scratches and polishing lines on cheek and neck and near ear and forehead to remove fine die pits.

Reverse D^2a– Two raised short bars with connecting lines between IT in UNITED from impressions of outside of denticles. Also shows the field edge line of denticle cavities at IT. Spacing between impressions matches denticle spacings. Fine die scratches in various directions on over polished tail feathers around eagle's right leg, between eagle's left wing and body and in middle of eagle's right wing. *Die markers–* Single polishing line up from eagle's right wing top up thru eagle's beak up to e in We, and polishing lines thru ST in STATES.

3GM IV I • D^2a (Scribbling Die Scratches #142, Denticle Impressions Wreath Top) (189) I-3 R-5

Reverse D^2a– Two raised short bars at top of right wreath from impressions of outside of denticles with denticle spacing of 0.030". Fine die scratches in various directions on over polished tail feathers around eagle's right leg and between eagle's left wing and body.

31(revised) **IV 25 • D^2a (Doubled Left Obverse, Scribbling Die Scratches) (189) I-2 R-5**

Obverse IV 25– All date digits doubled on left side. All left stars, E PLURI and forward edge of Liberty head hair slightly doubled towards rim.

Reverse D^2a– Fine die scratches in various directions on over polished tail feathers around eagle's right leg and between eagle's left wing and body. *Die marker–* Long diagonal polishing line at lower right inside of eagle's right leg feathers.

31A1 IV 25 • D^2a (Doubled Left Obv., Denticle Impressions Above Arrow Heads) (189) I-4 R-5

Reverse D^2a– Six raised triangles above arrow heads from impressions of outside of denticles, plus one below upper arrow head tip and two below lower arrow head. Spacing between triangles matches denticle spacings.

31A2 IV 25 • D^2a (Doubled Left Obv., Denticle Impressions Above Arrow Heads) (189) I-4 R-6

Obverse IV 25– Later die state shows die file/polishing lines in fields in front of nose, upper neck and above date to remove die clash marks.

Reverse D^2a– Later die state shows die file/polishing lines in upper right fields to remove die clash marks. Faint sixth right denticle impression has been removed.

31B IV 25 • D^2a (Dbld Left Obv., Denticle Impressions Above Arrow Heads, Below God) (189) I-4 R-5

Reverse D^2a– Three denticle impressions added below G in God in later die state.

40 IV 33 • D^1a (Quadrupled Right Stars) (189) I-2 R-5

Obverse IV 33– All right stars and 1–3 left stars slightly quadrupled towards rim. Doubled 4–7 left stars. Both 1's in date tripled towards rim and doubled 92.

40A IV 33 • D^1a (Quadrupled Right Stars, Denticle Impressions on Reverse) (189) I-4 R-5

Obverse IV 33– Some horizontal die polishing lines thru M of UNUM.

Reverse D^1a– Five raised triangles below left tail feathers from impressions of outside of denticles with some faint raised triangles above these five. Spacings between raised triangles matches denticle spacings.

1921 S

1AJ(reviseda0 **IV 1 • D^2a (Denticle & Die Edge Impressions Above Arrow Feathers) (189) I-3 R-5**

Obverse IV 1– Very slightly doubled and tripled left stars towards rim.

Reverse D^2a– Two raised triangular dots above arrow feathers from impressions of outside of denticles. Spacing between triangles matches denticle spacings. Short die scratch at end of top arrow feather below denticle impressions likely from die edge. Fine diagonal polishing lines around Trust. Some raised dots within and below right tail feathers from rusted die.

PHOTOGRAPHS OF DENTICLE IMPRESSIONS DIE VARIETIES

(New Added)

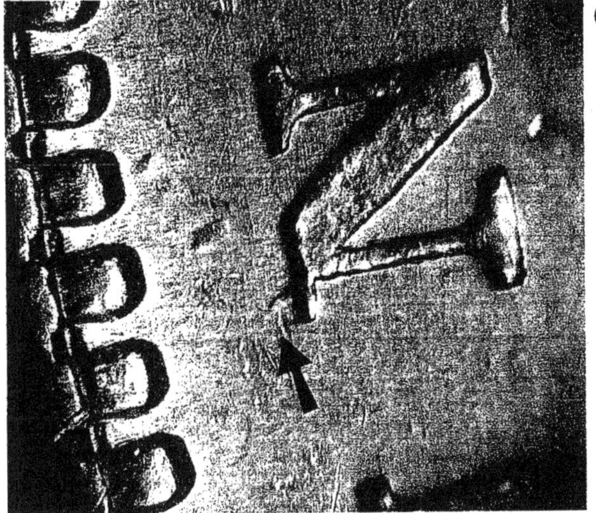

1878 S VAM 34A Three Denticle Space Impressions Rim- N of UNITED

1878 S VAM 34A Three Denticle Impressions Olive Leaf Cluster

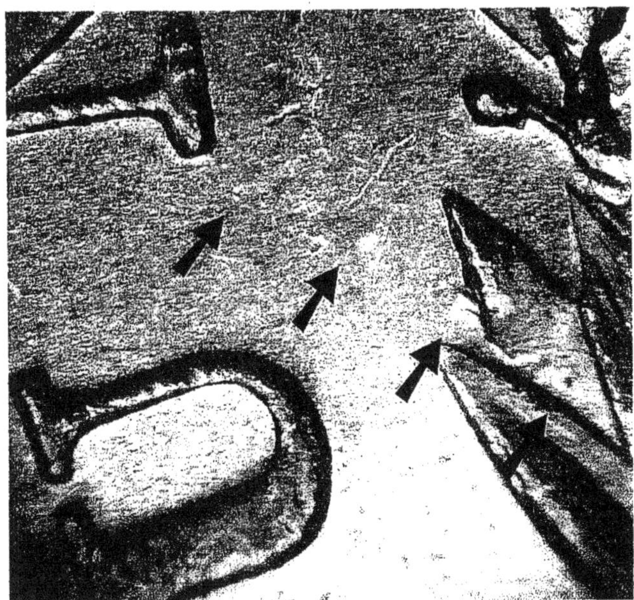

1878 S VAM 34A Four Denticle Impressions N– Wreath Leaf

1878 S VAM 34A Three Denticle Impressions U in United

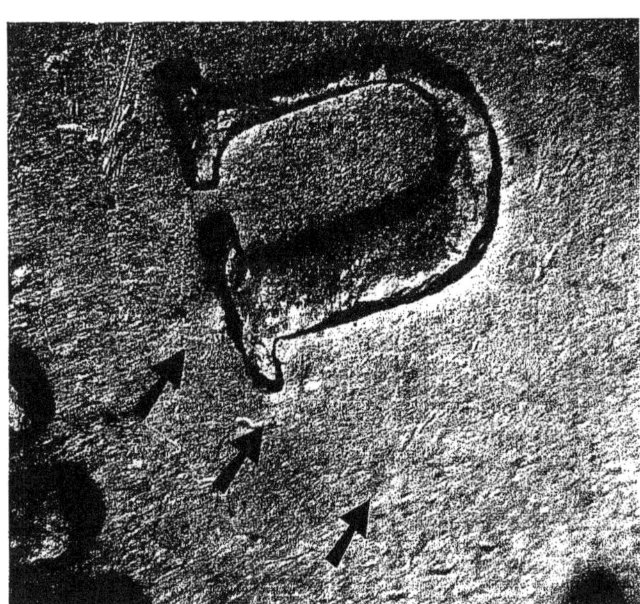

1878 S VAM 34A Three Denticle Impressions Wreath– Middle Olive Leaf Cluster

1878 S VAM 34A Three Denticle Impressions E of ONE

1878 S VAM 34 Die Flakes On Lower Hair

1884 P VAM 8J Denticle Impressions Leaf Edges

1884 P VAM 8J Die marker- Double Polishing Lines Below Cotton Boll

1884 P VAM 8J Die marker- Dots & Lines Wing-Neck Gap

1889 P VAM 1C1 Denticle Impressions Below TF

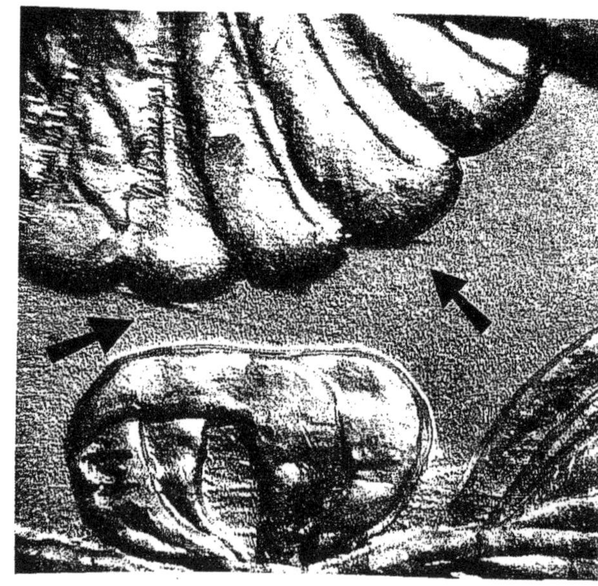
1889 P VAM 1C Possible Die Edge Lines

1889 P VAM 1E Four Denticle Impressions

1889 P VAM 1E Die marker- Polishing Line Ear Front

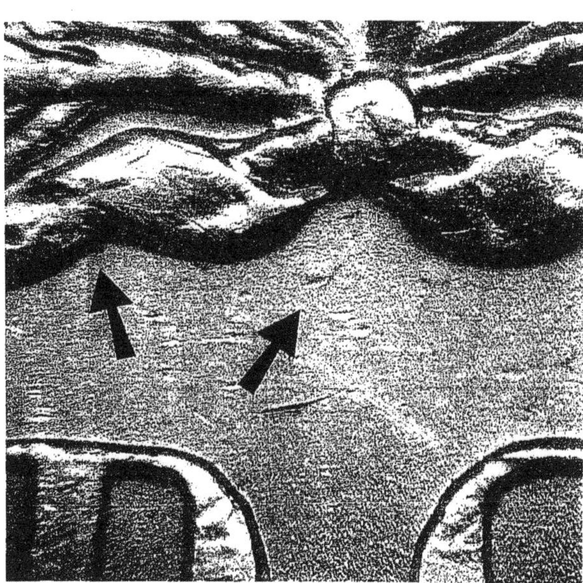
1889 P VAM 1F Denticle Impressions Below Wreath Bow

1889 P VAM 1E Die marker- Two Die Scratches Claw

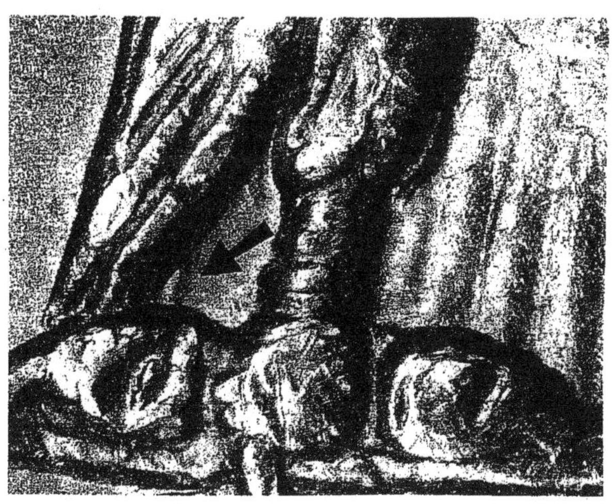
1889 P VAM 1F Die marker- Line Left of Eagle's Leg

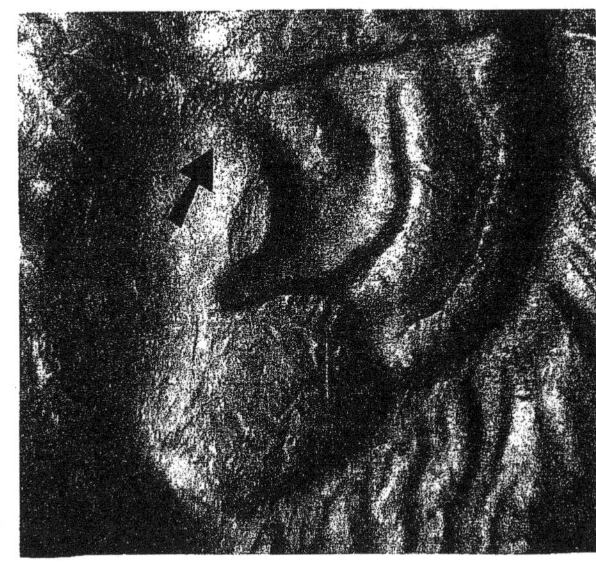
1889 P VAM 1F Die marker- Polishing Lines Top Left Ear

1889 P VAM 5E Possible Denticle Impressions & Die Edge Line

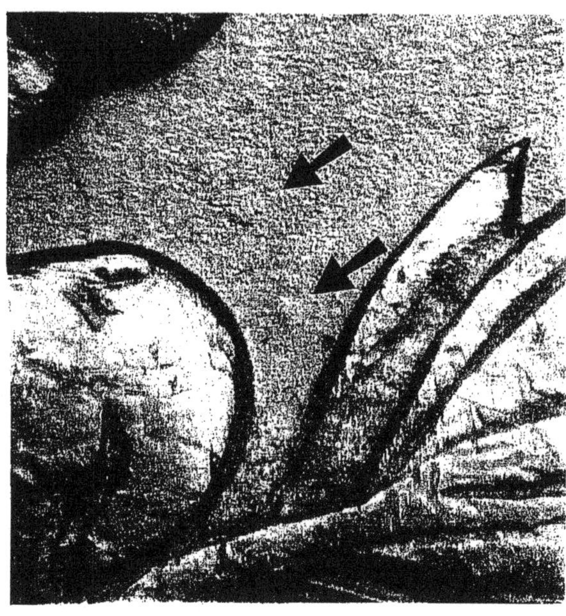

1889 P VAM 5E Two Denticle Impressions Bow

1889 P VAM 5E Die marker- Polishing Lines Jaw-Neck Junction

1889 P VAM 14 Doubled 18-9

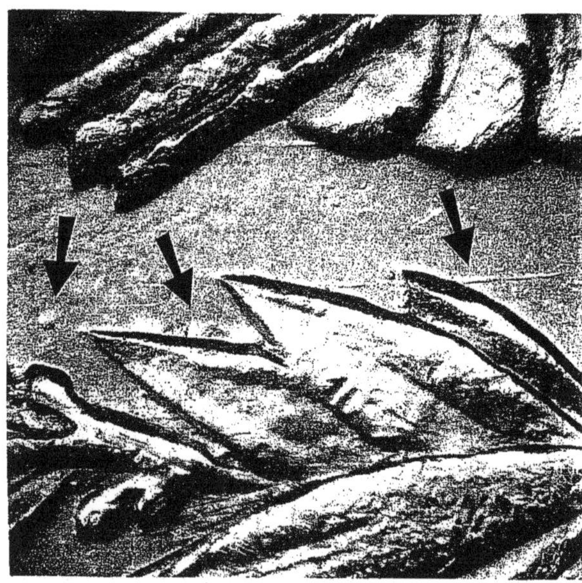

1889 P VAM 14A Denticle & Possible Die Edge Impressions Wreath Leaves

1889 P VAM 14A Denticle Impressions Below TF

1889 P VAM 62 Three Denticle Impressions,
Lines Wreath Bow

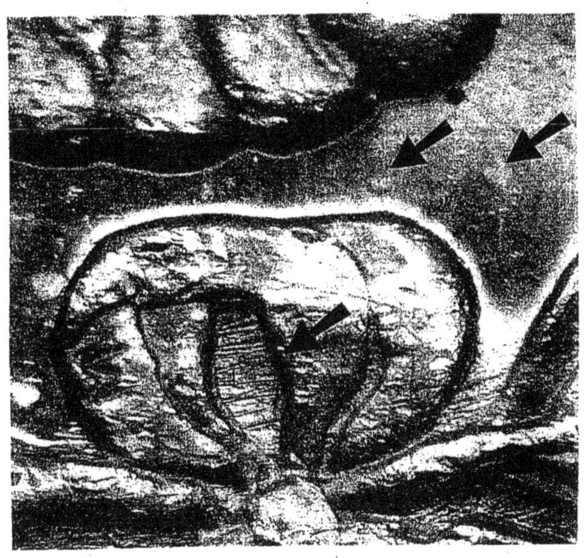

1889 P VAM 62 Two Denticle Impressions,
Lines Wreath Bow

1889 P VAM 62 Three Denticle Impressions Berries

1889 P VAM 62 Far Date, High 9

1889 P VAM 62 Die marker- Line Back of Neck

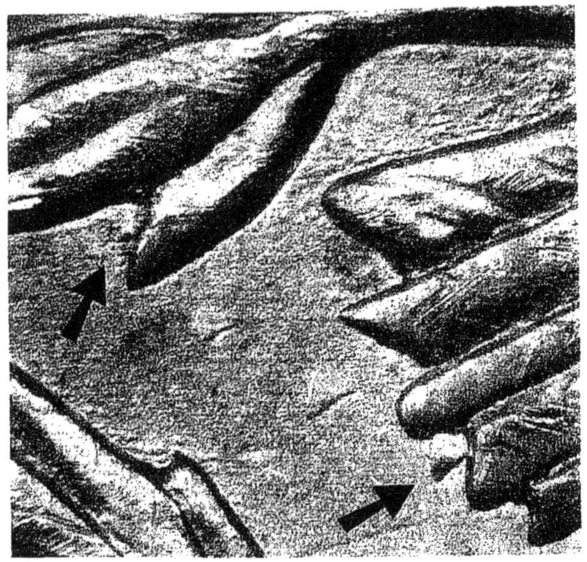

1889 O VAM 9C Four Triangular Denticle Impressions

1889 O VAM 9C Possible Die Edge Impressions Leg

1889 O VAM 9C Possible Curved Die Edge Impression

1889 O VAM 9C Die marker- Horizontal Polishing Line Middle TF

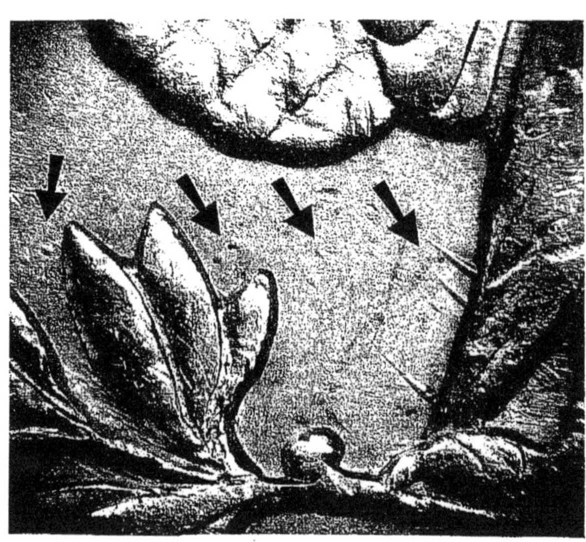

1890 O VAM 1H Denticle & Possible Die Edge Impressions

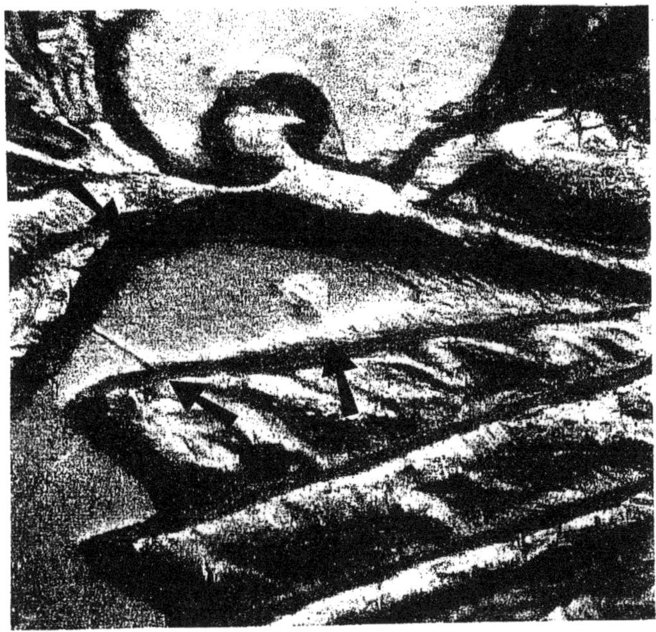

1890 O VAM 1 I Two Denticle Impressions & Die Edge Line

1890 O VAM 1 I Die marker- Die Chip Upper TF

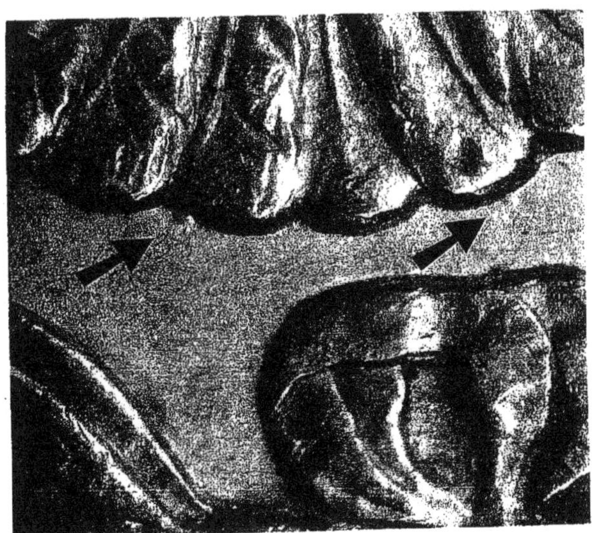

1890 O VAM 2D Two Possible Denticle Impressions TF

1890 O VAM 2D Two Die Gouges Wing-Body

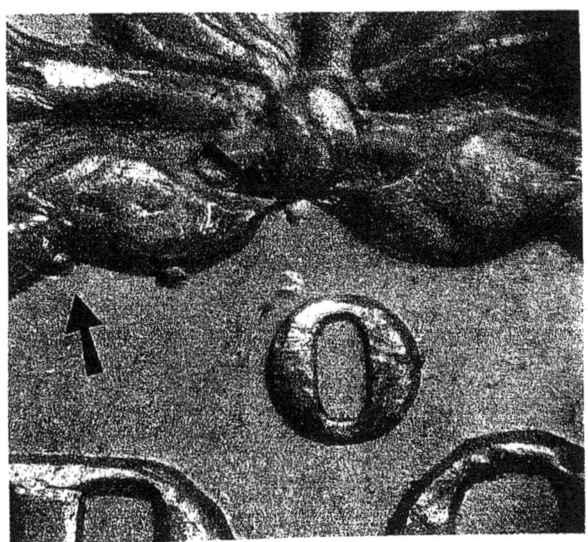

1890 O VAM 16B Denticle Impressions Below Ribbon

1890 O VAM 16B Die marker- Small Die Gouge Ear

1890 O VAM 28B Denticle Impressions Wreath Bow

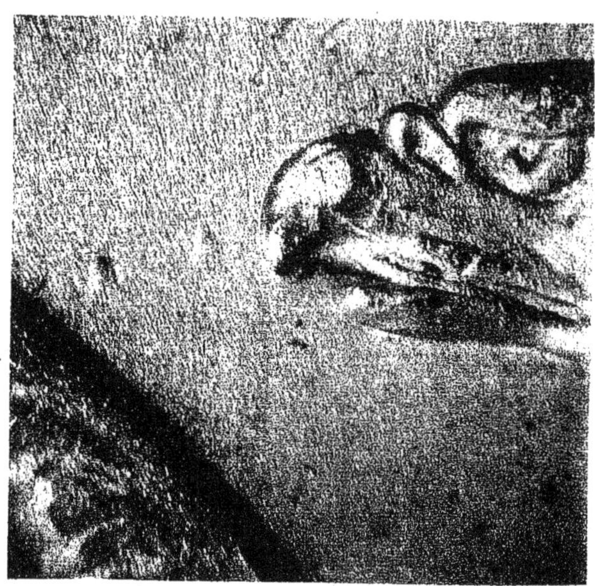

1891 P VAM 6B Denticle Impressions Eagle's Beak

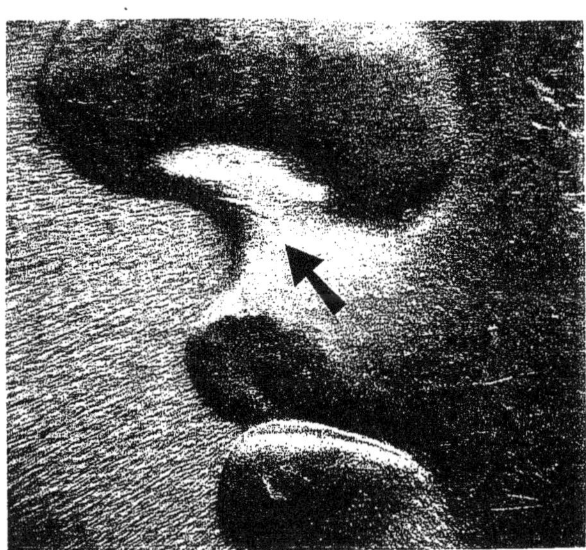

1891 P VAM 6B Die marker- Thread-Like Line Below Nostril

1900 O VAM 35 Doubled 900, Possible Denticle Impressions Hair Edge

1900 O VAM 35 Near Date With Die Cracks, Possible Denticle Impressions

1900 O VAM 35 Doubled Ear

1900 O VAM 35 Die marker- Polishing Line Inner Feather

1900 O VAM 35A Clashed n

1900 O VAM 47B Dots on 900

1900 O VAM 47B Three Denticle Impressions DO

1900 O VAM 47B Die Gouges Eagle's Wing-Leg

1900 O VAM 47B Die Scratches Wing Middle

1900 O VAM 47B Slightly Doubled UNITED

1902 O VAM 90 2 Top In Denticles

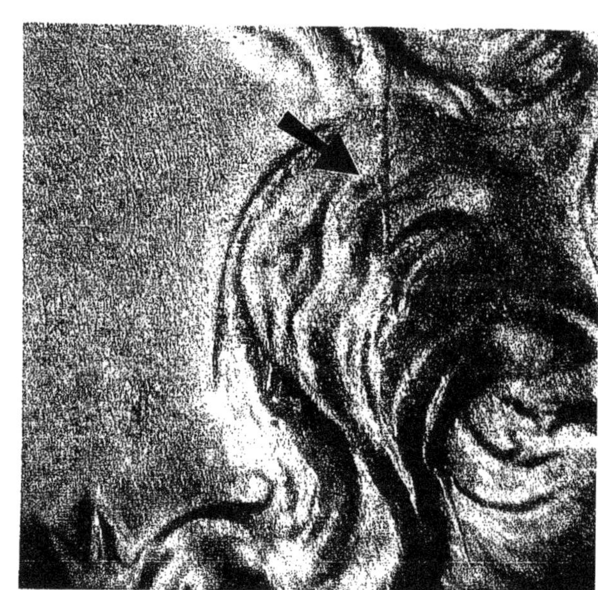

1902 O VAM 90 Die marker- Vertical Die Scratch Hair

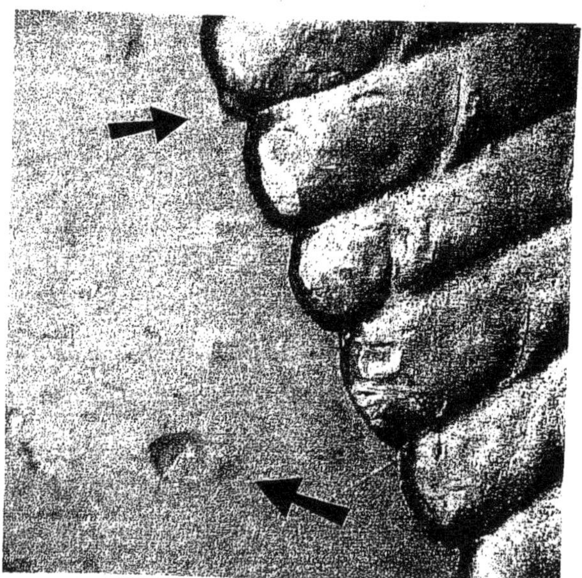

1902 O VAM 90A Denticle Impressions Wing Edge

1902 O VAM 90 Die marker- Die Rust Pits AR

1921 P VAM 3GM Scribbling Wing-Body

1921 P VAM 3GM Two Denticle Impressions Wreath Top

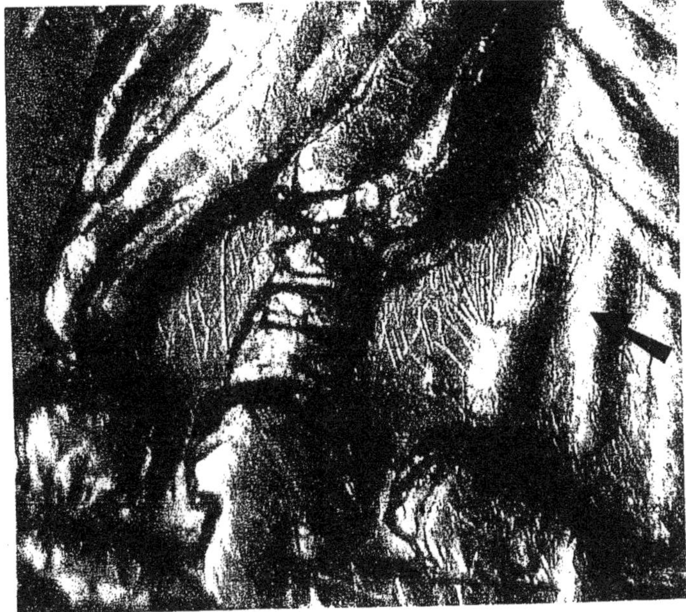

1921 P VAM 3GM Scribbling Die Scratches Leg

PHOTOGRAPHS OF DENTICLE IMPRESSIONS DIE VARIETIES

(Previously Listed)

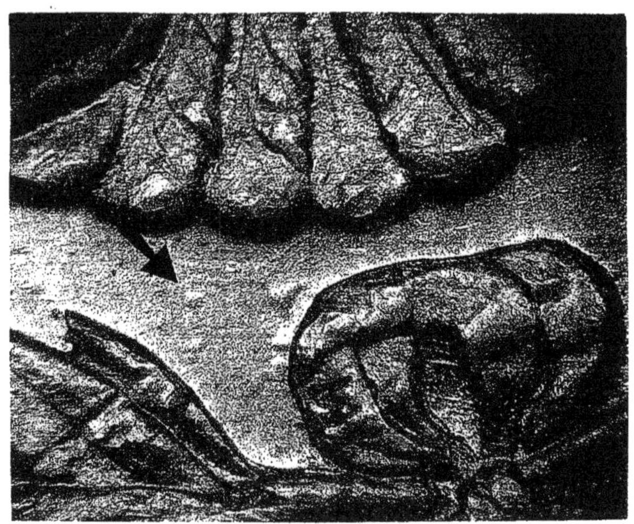

1878 P VAM 221A Denticle Impressions

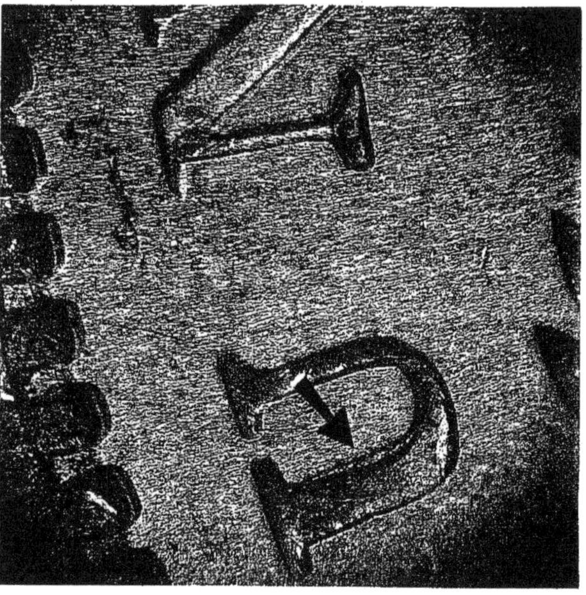

1878 P VAM 221 C^3b Doubled Left Reverse, U

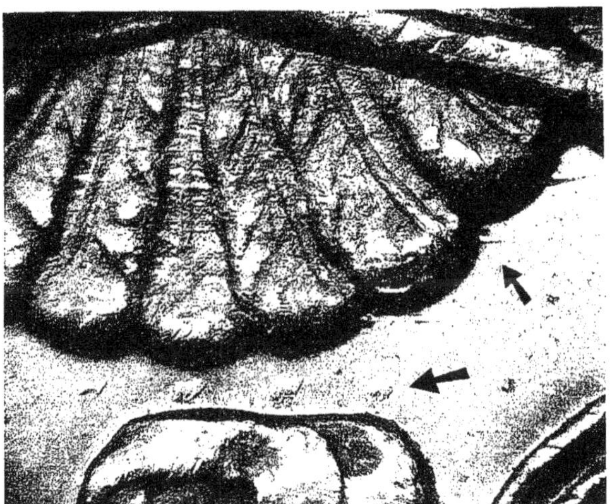

1878 P VAM 225A Denticle Impressions

1878 P VAM 225A Spiked Eye

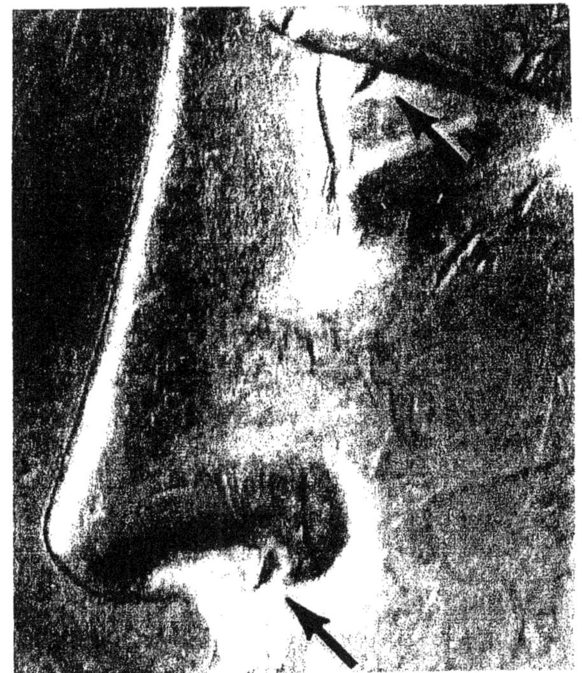

1878 CC VAM 20 Die Gouge Eye, Nostril

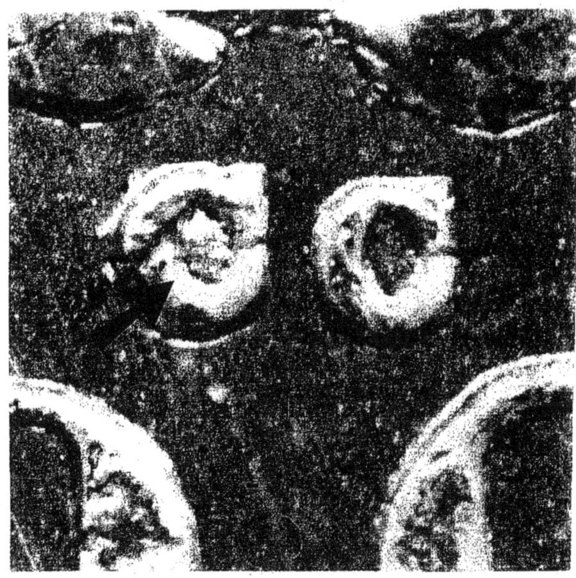

1878 CC VAM 20 Die Chip Left C

1878 CC VAM 20A Denticle Impressions TA

1878 CC VAM 20 Polishing Lines

1878 S VAM 17 Doubled D

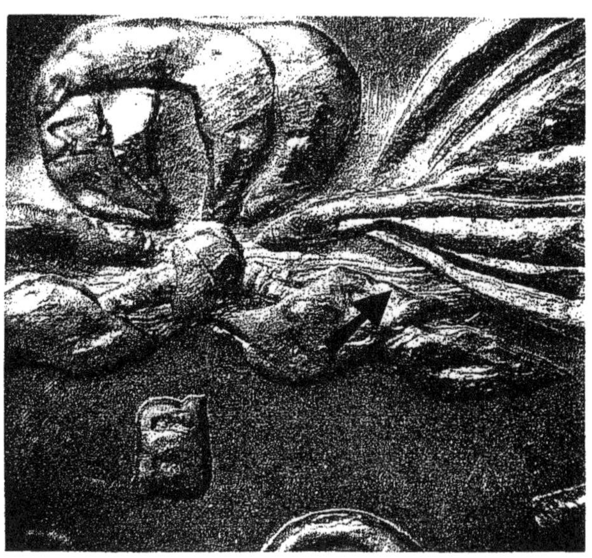

1878 S VAM 17 Die Gouge Ribbon

1878 S VAM 17A Over Polished Hair

1878 S VAM 17A Denticle Impressions Below TF

1878 S VAM 17A Denticle Impressions OLL

1878 S VAM 17A Lengthened Denticle Spaces, R

1878 S VAM 17B Denticle Impressions Neck

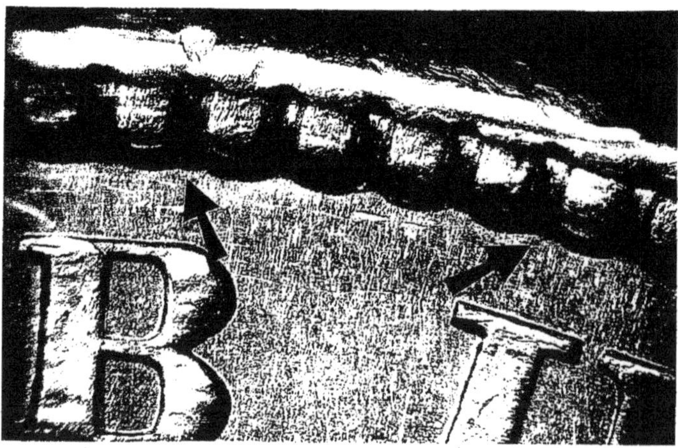

1878 S VAM 17A Lengthened Denticle Spaces, BU

1878 S VAM 17B Denticle Impressions Date

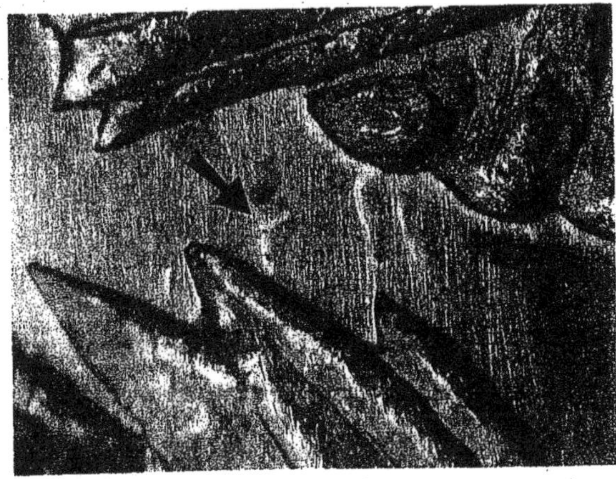
1878 S VAM 17B Denticle Impressions Below TF

1878 S VAM 17B Denticle Lines Above ST

1878 S VAM 17B Denticle Impressions AT

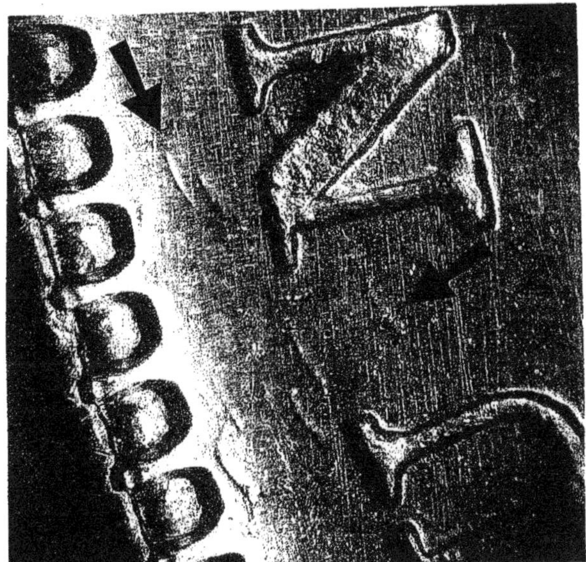
1878 S VAM 17B Denticle Impressions UN

1878 S VAM 17B Denticle Impressions OLL

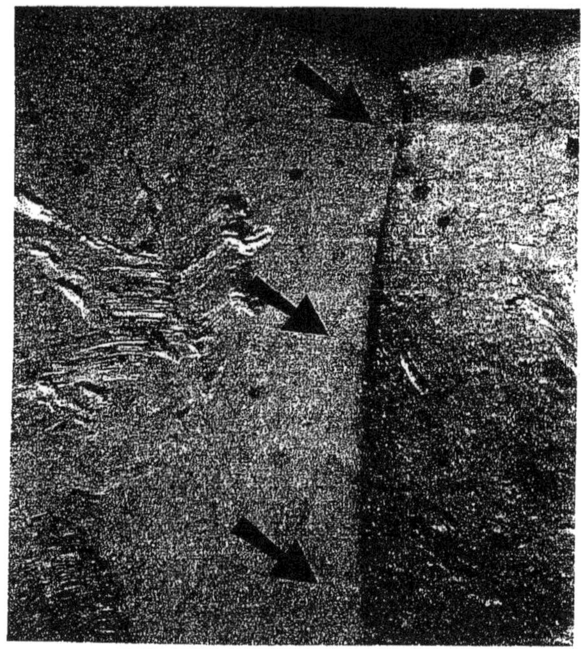

1878 S VAM 17C Denticle Impressions Neck

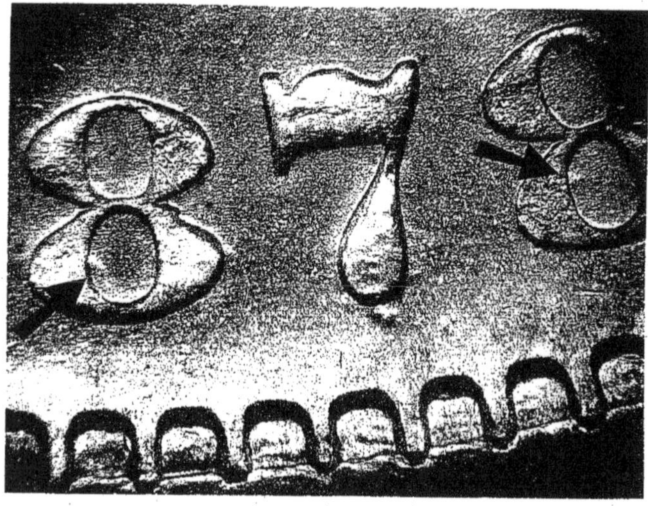

1878 S VAM 17C Denticle Impressions at Date

1878 S VAM 17C Denticle Impressions Above St

1878 S VAM 17C Denticle Impressions AT

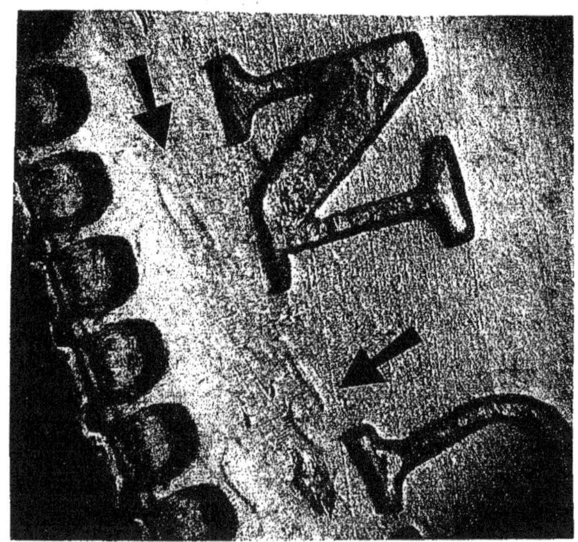

1878 S VAM 17C Denticle Impressions UN

1878 S VAM 17C Denticle Impressions OLL

1879 P VAM 57 Doubled 18

1879 P VAM 57 Doubled 79

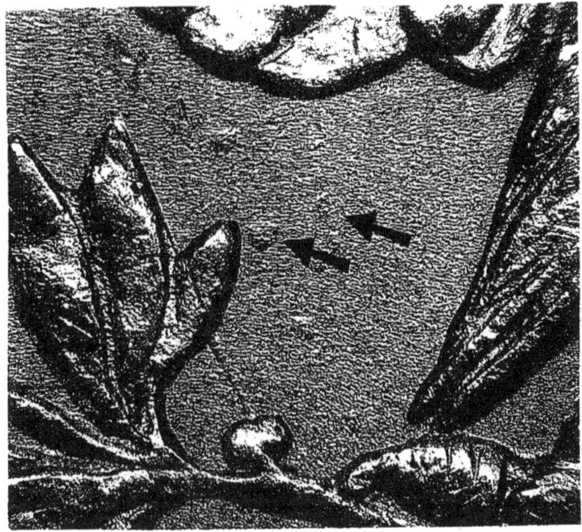

1879 P VAM 57A Denticle & Die Edge Impressions

1881 O VAM 18A Denticle & Die Edge Impressions

1883 O VAM 2A Denticle Impressions In

1883 O VAM 2A Denticle Impressions S

1886 O VAM 1C Raised Triangular Dot

1887 P VAM 1E Denticle Impressions

1888 P VAM 1D Denticle Impressions

1888 P VAM 1D Die Scratch Tail Feathers

1888 P VAM 17A Denticle Impressions Left

1888 P VAM 17A Denticle Impressions Rt.

1889 P VAM 5D Denticle Impressions Arrow Feathers

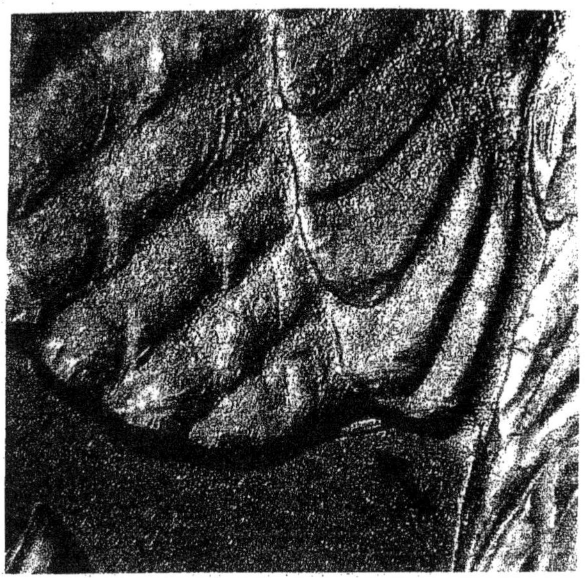

1889 P VAM 5D Die marker-
Die Gouge Wing Bottom

1889 P VAM 18B Denticle Impressions
Below Arrow Feathers

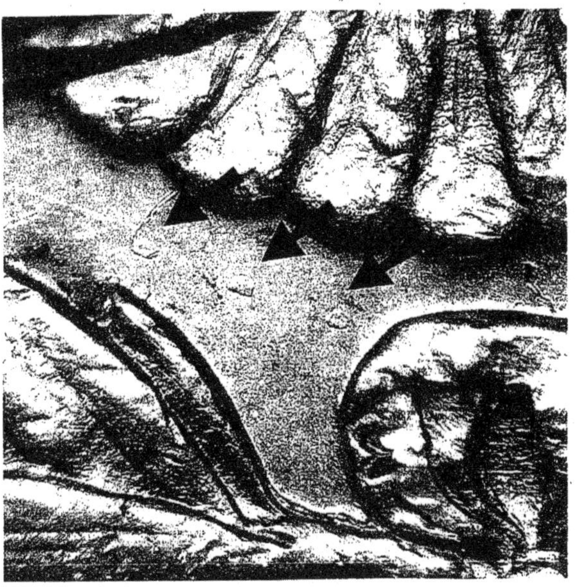

1889 O VAM 9B Denticle Impressions

1889 O VAM 13F Denticle Impressions

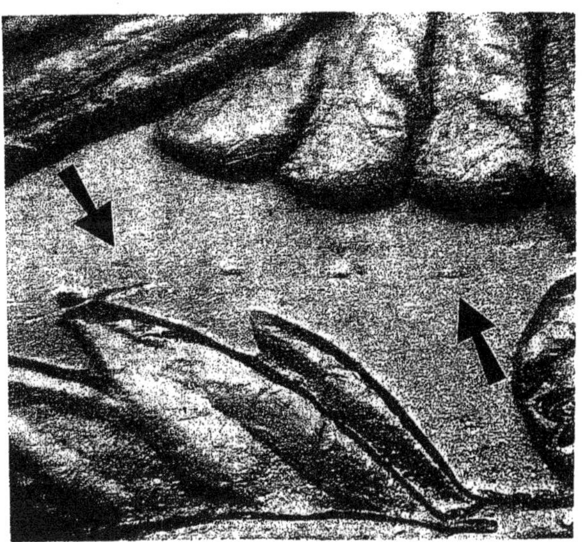

1889 O VAM 16A Denticle Impressions

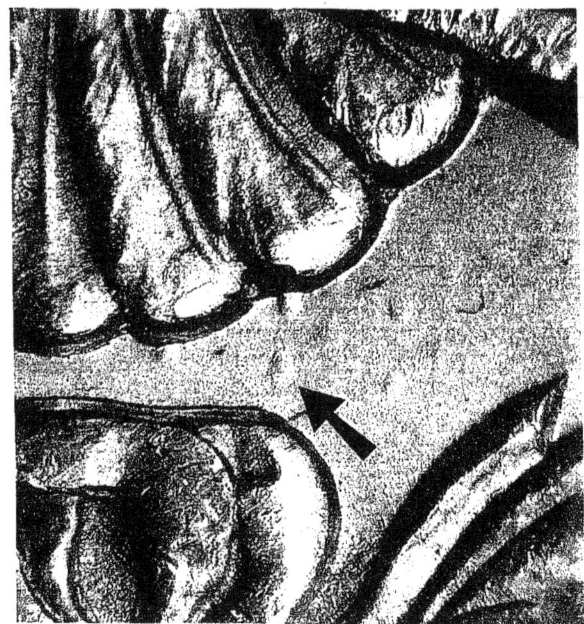

1890 P VAM 1C Denticle Impressions

1890 P VAM 1D Polishing Lines Wreath Bow

1890 P VAM 1D Denticle & Die Edge Impressions

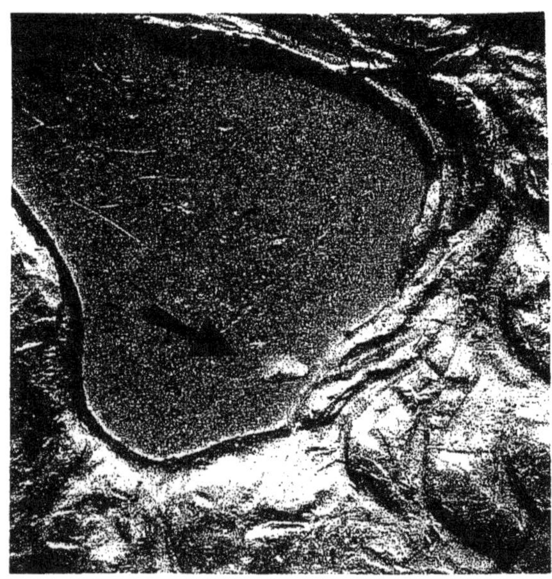

1890 P VAM 1E Denticle Impressions
Eagle's Rt. Shoulder

1890 P VAM 1E Denticle Impression
Below Arrow Feather

1890 P VAM 1F Denticle Impressions Rt. Of Leg

1890 P VAM 1F Denticle Impressions Below TF

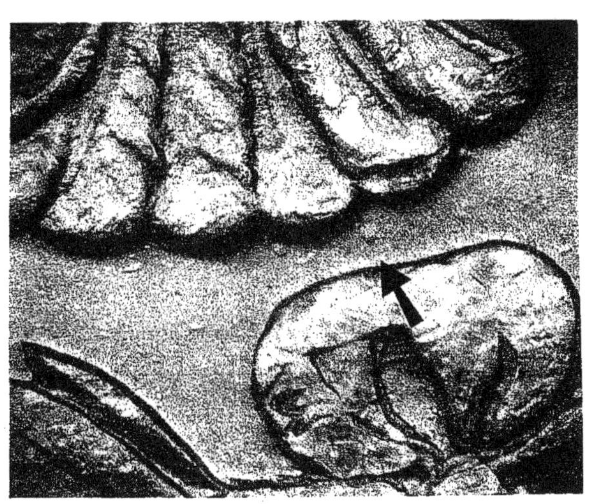

1890 P VAM 1G Denticle Impressions Middle TF

1890 P VAM 1I Denticle Impressions Wreath Bow

1890 P VAM 4A Denticle Impressions

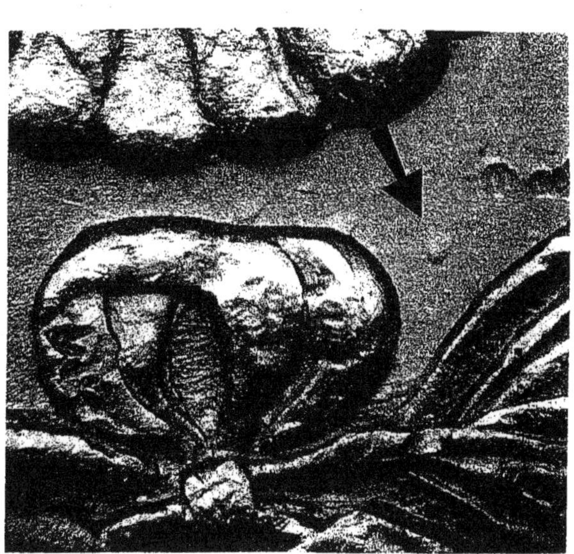

1890 P VAM 11A Denticle Impressions Wreath Bow

1890 O VAM 1C Denticle Impressions

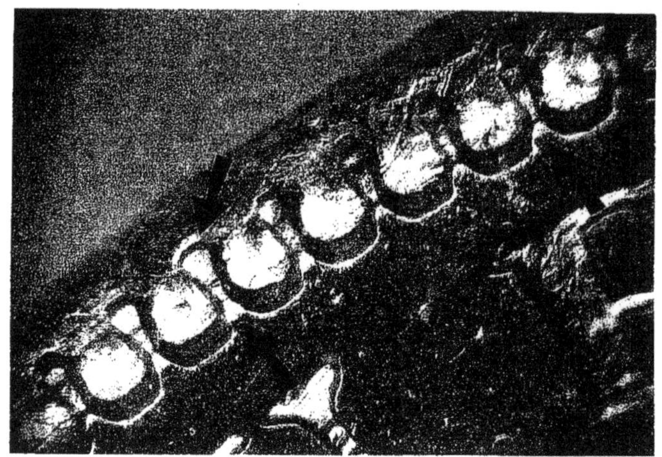

1890 O VAM 1C Obverse Denticle Spaces

1890 O VAM 1G Denticle Impressions Arrow Feathers

1890 O VAM 33A Denticle Impressions
Below Olive Leaves

1890 O VAM 33A Denticle Impressions
Arrow Feathers

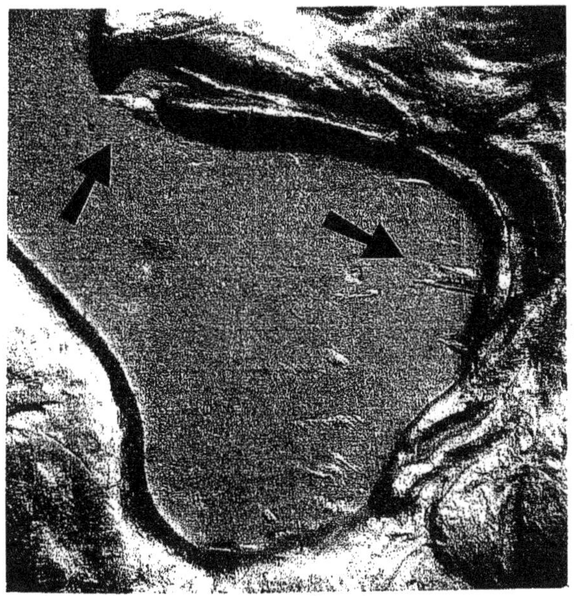

1890 O VAM 33 Gouges Mouth & Neck

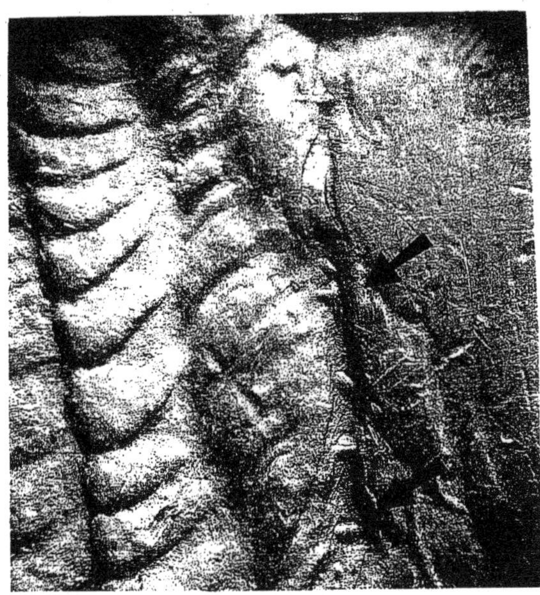

1890 O VAM 33 Gouges Wing-Body Junction

1890 O VAM 33 Gouges Below Wing

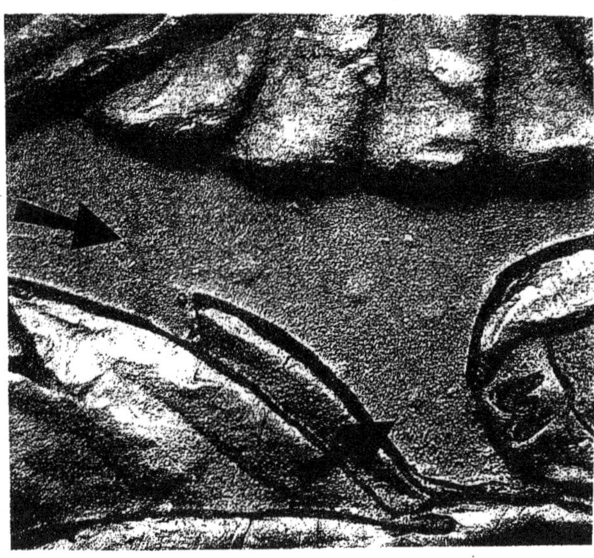

1891 P VAM 1B Denticle Impressions

1891 P VAM 1B Denticle Impressions

1891 P VAM 6A Denticle Impressions Below TF

1891 O VAM 5A Denticle Impressions

1891 O VAM 5 O/O Top

1894 O VAM 11 Low Date

1894 O VAM 11A Clashed D

1894 O VAM 11B Denticle Impressions, Die Clashes

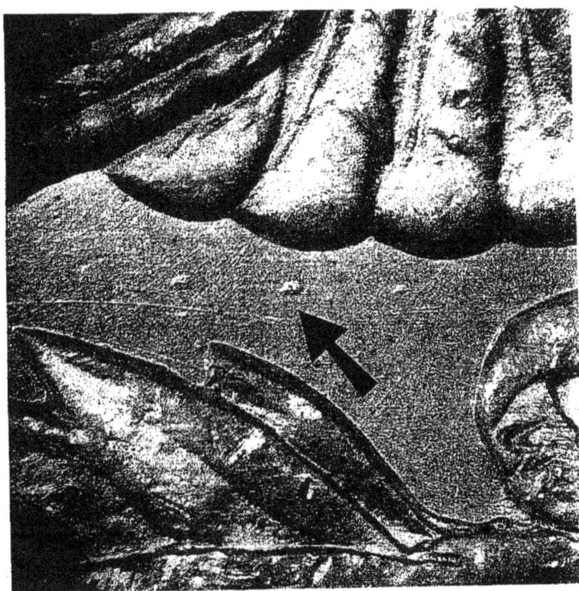

1900 O VAM 21E Denticle Impressions

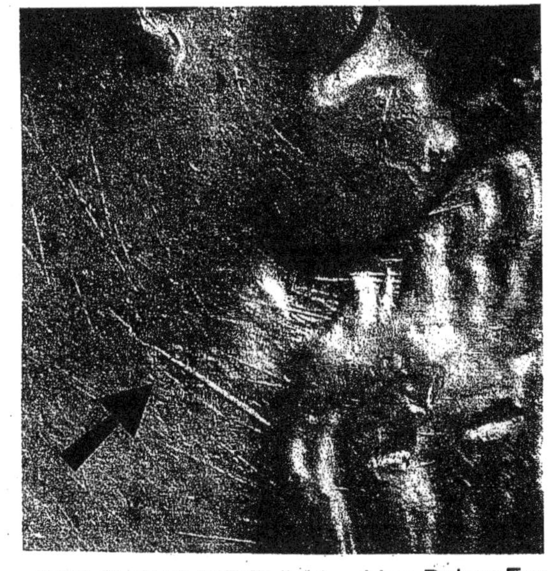

1900 O VAM 21E Polishing Line Below Ear

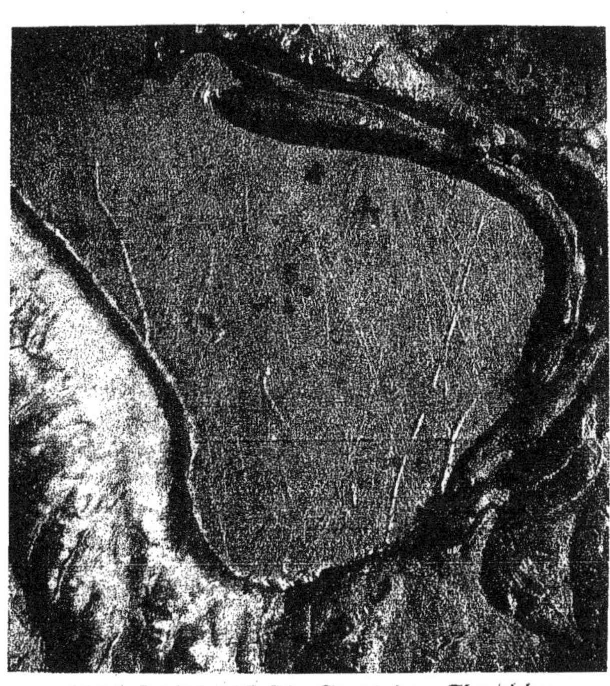

1901 O VAM 1B Die Scratches Shoulder

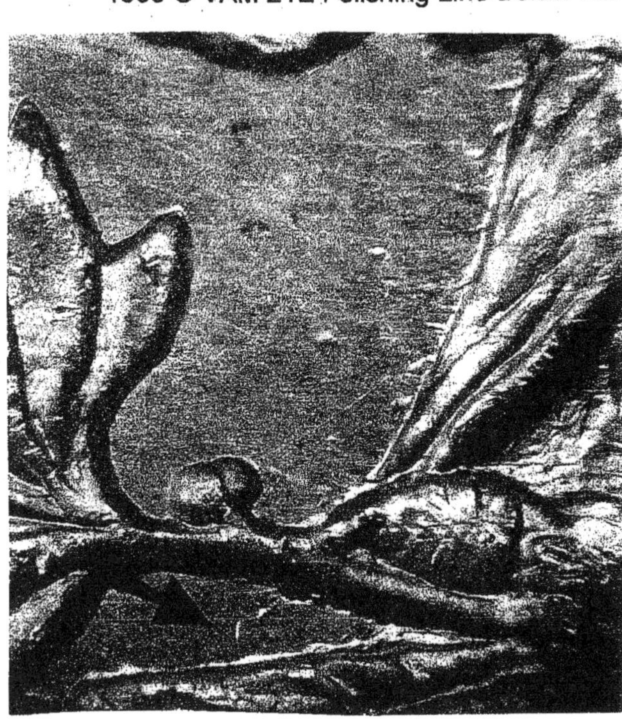

1901 O VAM 1B Denticle Impression Arrow Feather

1901 O VAM 11 Die Scratch Below Eye

1901 O VAM 11 Two Die Scratches Wreath

1901 O VAM 11A Denticle Impressions Arrow Heads

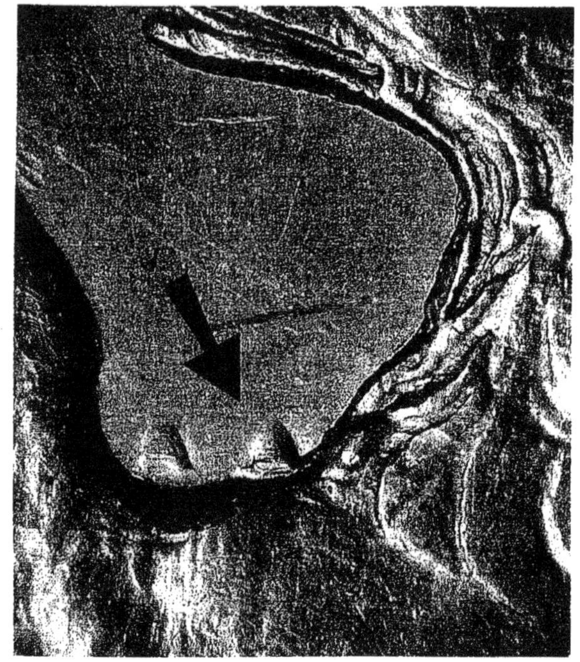

1901 O VAM 45 Two Denticle Impressions

1901 O VAM 45 2 Olive Reverse, 2 Die Gouges

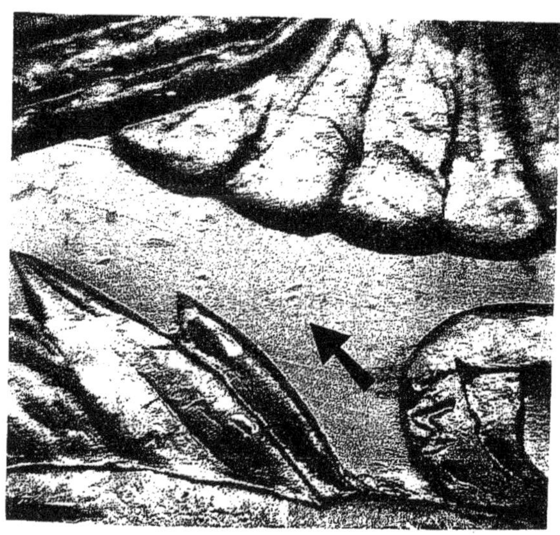

1902 O VAM 44B Denticle Impressions Below TF

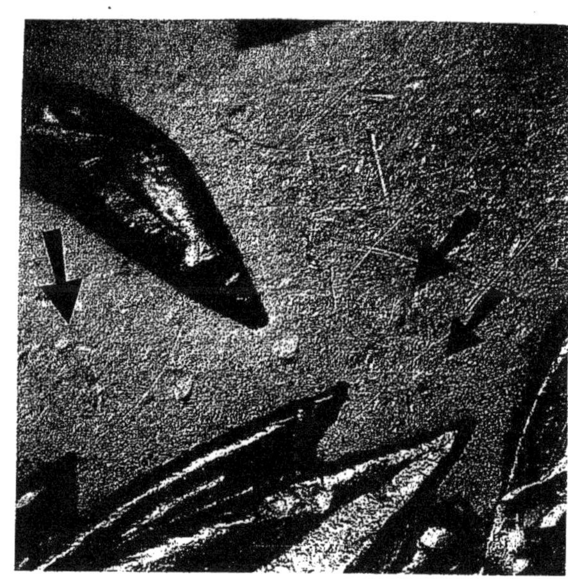

1903 P VAM 1B Denticle Impressions
Olive Branch

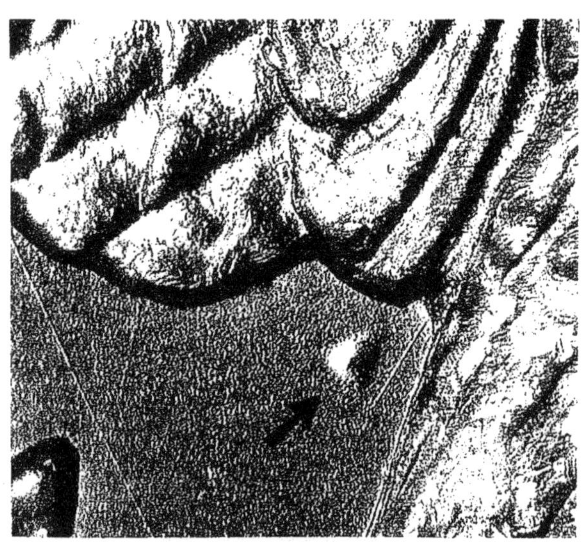

1904 O VAM 12 Denticle Impression
Early 2nd Die Combo

1904 O VAM 12 Denticle Impression
Late 2nd Die Combo

1904 O VAM 12 Doubled 9

1904 O VAM 12 Doubled 4

1904 O VAM 12 Die Scratch Eye Front

1904 O VAM 22A1 Denticle Impression Below Wing

1904 O VAM 22A2 Die Gouge O

1904 O VAM 22A2 Denticle Impression, Late Stage, 3rd Die Combo

1904 O VAM 22A2 Lines in TY

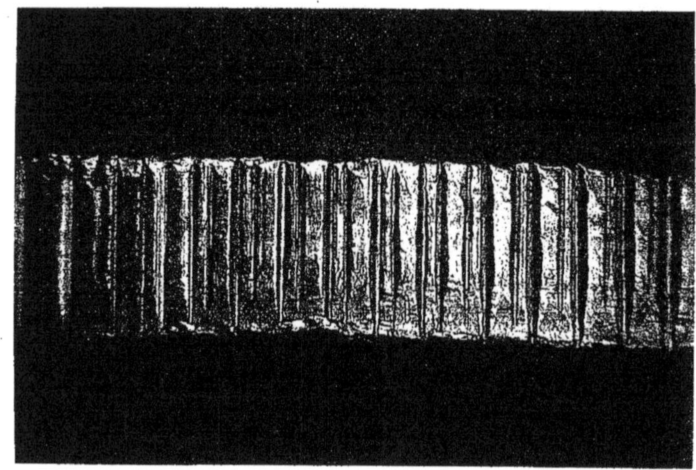
1904 O VAM 22A2 Overlapping Reeding 12 O'clock

1904 O VAM 30A Denticle Impressions

1904 O VAM 22A2 Overlapping Reeding 7:30 O'clock

1904 O VAM 30B Denticle Impressions E-D

1904 O VAM 30B Die Scratches Wing Edge

1921 P VAM 3F1 Die Gouge Wing

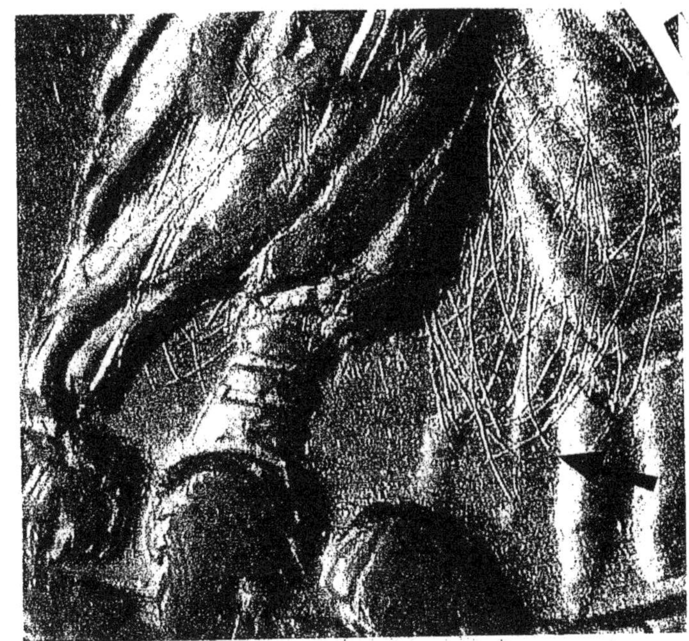

1921 P VAM 3F1 Scribbling Die Scratches

1921 VAM 3F1 Scribbling Wing-Body

1921 P VAM 3F1 Scribbling Wing Middle

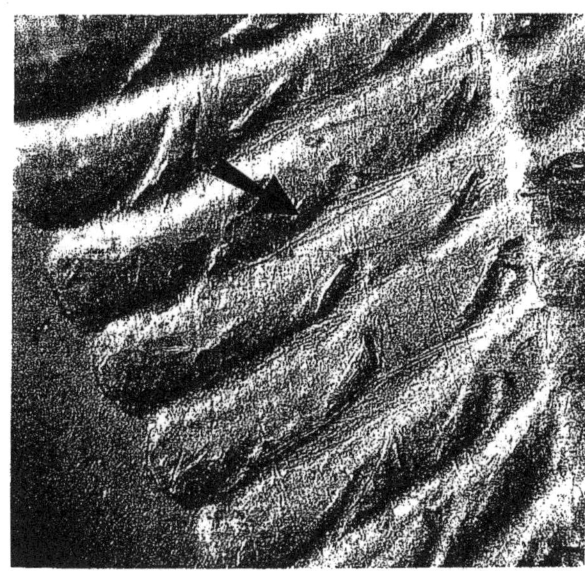

1921 P VAM 3F1 Scribbling Wing Middle

1921 P VAM 3F1 Denticle Impressions ME

1921 P VAM 3F2 Denticle Impressions ME

1921 P VAM 3F3 Pitted Reverse

1921 P VAM 3F4 Die Break R

1921 P VAM 3F3 Denticle Impressions ME

1921 P VAM 3ER Denticle Impressions IT

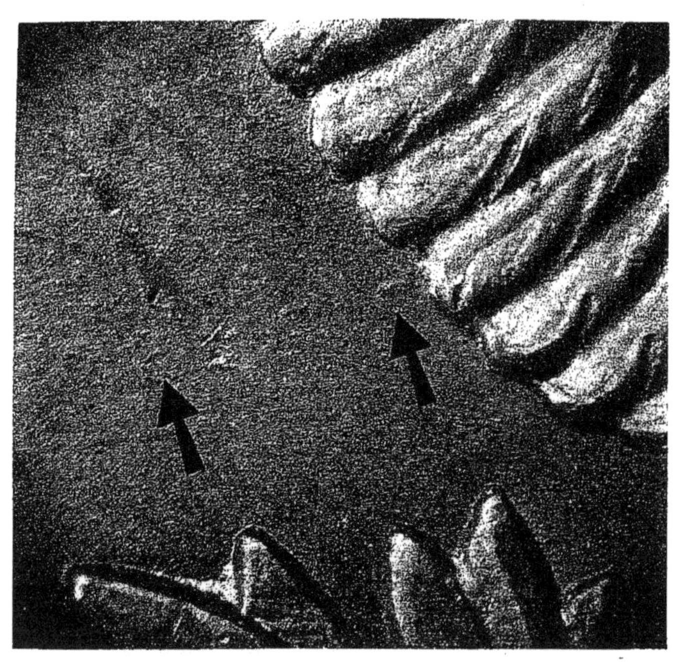

1921 P VAM 3CW2 Denticle Impressions Wing

1921 P VAM 3ER Scribbling Die Scratches

1921 P VAM 3ER Scribbling Wing-Body

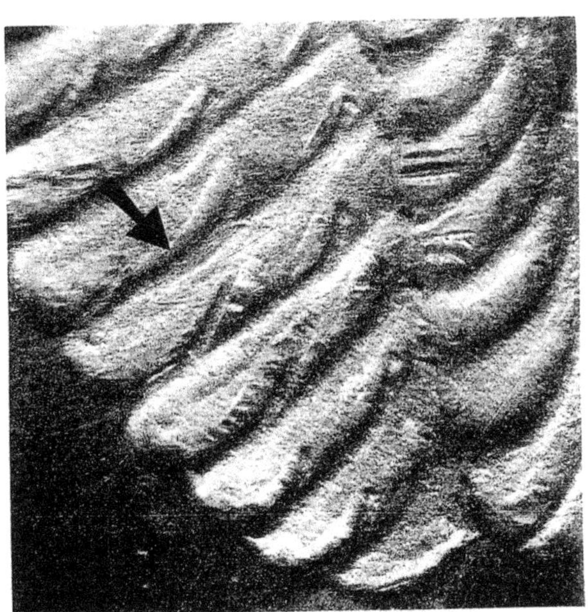

1921 P VAM 3ER Scribbling Wing Middle

1921 P VAM 3ER Polishing Lines ST

1921 P VAM 3ER Polishing Line Beak

1921 P VAM 3ER Scribbling Die Scratches Cheek

1921 P VAM 31 Scribbling Die Scratches

1921 P VAM 31 Scribbling Wing-Body

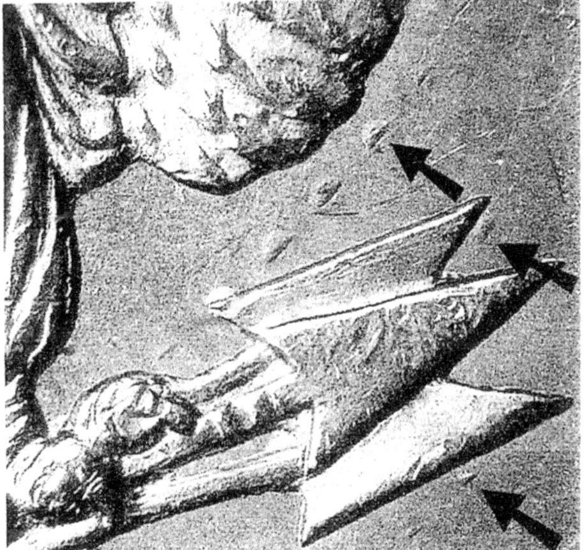
1921 P VAM 31A1 Denticle Impressions

1921 P VAM 31 Doubled Left Obverse

1921 P VAM 31A2 Die File Lines Obverse

1921 P VAM 31B Two Denticle Impressions

1921 P VAM 40A Denticle Impressions

1921 P VAM 40A Quadrupled Right Stars

1921 S VAM 1AJ Denticle &
Die Edge Impressions

1921 S VAM 1AJ Rust Pits

1879 P VAM 57A Denticle & Die Edge Impressions

1881 O VAM 18A Denticle & Die Edge Impressions

1890 P VAM 1D Denticle & Die Edge Impressions

1890 O VAM 1 I Two Denticles & Die Edge Impressions

1921 S VAM 1AJ Two Denticles & Die Edge Impressions

1889 P VAM 5E Possible Denticle & Die Edge Impressions

1889 P VAM 5E Two Denticle Impressions Wreath Bow

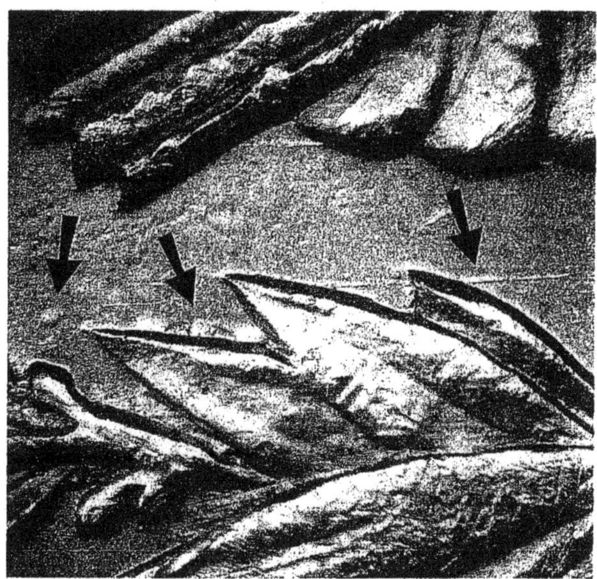

1889 P VAM 14A Denticle & Possible Die Edge Impressions Wreath Leaves

1889 P VAM 14A Denticle Impressions Below TF

1890 O VAM 1H Denticle & Possible Die Edge Impressions

1889 O VAM 9C Four Triangular Denticle Impressions

1889 O VAM 9C Possible Curved Die Edge Impression

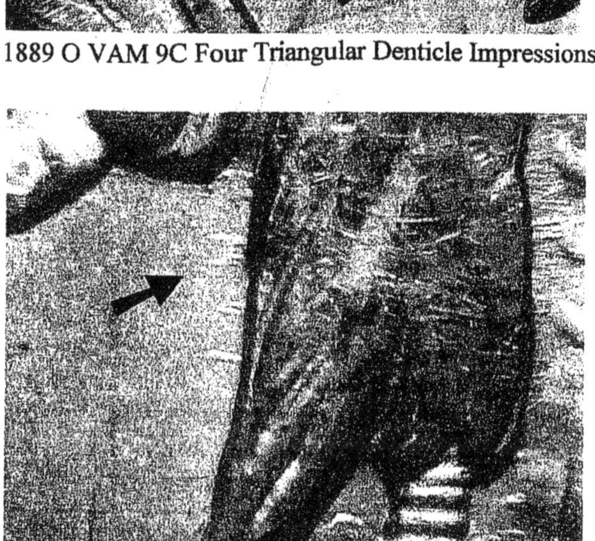
1889 O VAM 9C Possible Die Edge Lines Eagle's Right Leg

1878 P VAM 7 Possible Die Edge Line A

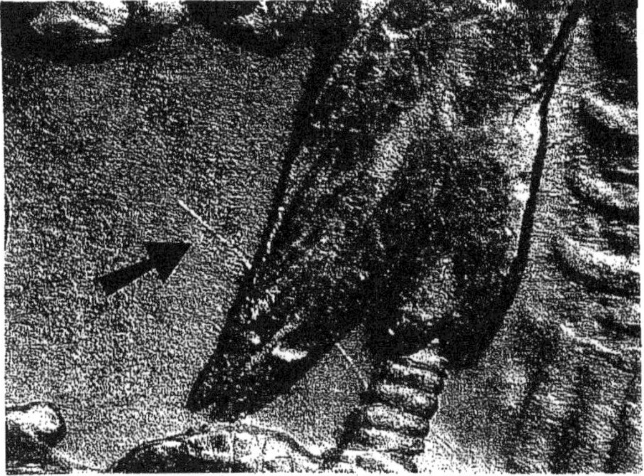

1879 P VAM 61 Possible Die Edge Line Leg

1884 CC VAM 4A Possible Die Edge Line E

1887 P VAM 26A Possible Die Edge Line A

1921 P VAM 1C/48 Possible Die Edge Line Wreath Bow

1921 P VAM 3H Possible Die Edge Line Olive Leaves

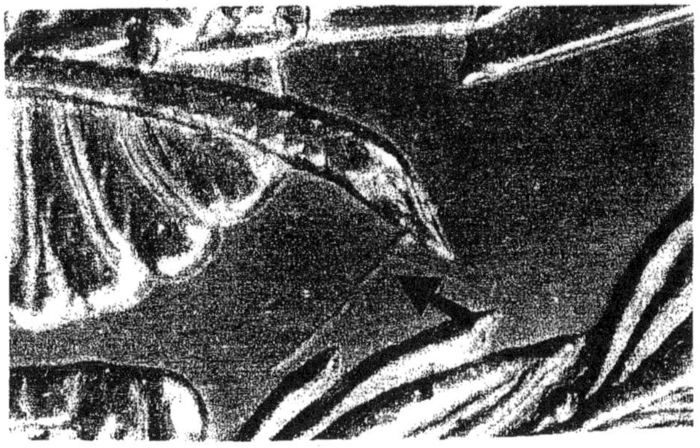

1921 P VAM 16 Possible Die Edge Line Olive Branch

1921 D VAM 1S Possible Die Edge Lines ED

1921 D VAM 1AA Possible Die Edge Line E

1921 D VAM 1AU Possible Die Edge Line N

1921 D VAM 1BD Possible Die Edge Line Wreath

1921 S VAM 1CE Possible Die Edge Line Below O

1921 S VAM 21B Possible Die Edge Line D

FURTHER REFERENCES

Please check Amazon Kindle for Michael S. Fey, Ph.D., and Leroy Van Allen & A. George Mallis publications. For hard copy print of books, please contact Dr. Fey at RCI, P.O. Box C, Ironia, NJ 07845 or eMail: Feyms@aol.com.

Hard copy books are also available at *The Institute for Silver Dollar Education and Research*, at website: *Ilovesilver dollars.org* or by contacting Executive Director John Baumgart at John.Baumgart@comcast.net

Amazon Kindle

Fey, Michael S. 2019. *The Complete Virtual Guide to Pricing Your Morgan Silver Dollars*. 286 pp. RCI

Van Allen, Leroy, & A. George Mallis. 2023. *Part I or II or III of Three. Comprehensive Catalog and Encyclopedia or Morgan & Peace Dollars*. RCI Total 520 pp.

Leroy Van Allen. 2011. *Wonders of Morgan Dollars*. 139 pp. RCI

Leroy Van Allen. 2013. *Wonders of Peace Dollars*. 273 pp. RCI

Leroy Van Allen. 2006. *Morgan Dollars 8 & 7 Over 8 Tail Feather Story*. 52 pp. RCI

Leroy Van Allen. 2010. *1878 P 7 Tail Feather Morgan Dollar Attribution Guide*. 130 pp. RCI

Leroy Van Allen. 2006. *1878 S Morgan Dollar Attribution Guide*. 139 pp. RCI

Fey, Michael S. 2009 The Top 100 Morgan Dollar Varieties: The VAM Keys

FURTHER REFERENCES

Hard Copy Books

Fey, Michael S. 2019. The Top 100 Morgan Dollar Varieties: The VAM Keys. 286 pp. RCI

Fey, Michael S. 2008. *A Decade of Top 100 Insights*. RCI 174 pp.

Van Allen, Leroy. 1991. *RotaFlip Die Rotation Booklet and Guide*. 1991. RCI

Kimpton, M.D., Mark. 2005. *Elite Clashed Morgan Dollars*. RCI 160 pp

Van Allen, Leroy, & A. George Mallis. 2023. *Comprehensive Catalog and Encyclopedia or Morgan & Peace Dollars*. RCI Total 520 pp.

Van Allen, Leroy 2011. *Wonders of Morgan Dollars*. 139 pp. RCI

Van Allen, Leroy 2013. *Wonders of Peace Dollars*. 273 pp. RCI

Van Allen, Leroy 2006. *Morgan Dollars 8 & 7 Over 8 Tail Feather Story*. 52 pp. RCI

Van Allen, Leroy 2010. *1878 P 7 Tail Feather Morgan Dollar Attribution Guide*. 130 pp. RCI

Van Allen, Leroy 2006. *1878 S Morgan Dollar Attribution Guide*. 139 pp. RCI

Van Allen, Leroy 2013. *Die Gouges and Scratches Peace Dollar Attribution Guide. 109 pp* RCI

Van Allen, Leroy 2008. *1921 Scribbles Morgan Dollar Attribution Guide*. 234 pp. RCI

Van Allen, Leroy. 2013. *Misplaced Date Digits Morgan Dollar Attribution Guide*. 57 pp RCI

Van Allen, Leroy. 2017. *Dashed Under 8 Morgan Dollar Attribution Guide*. 53 pp. RCI

Van Allen, Leroy. 2009. *Overdates and Over Mint Marks of Morgan Dollar Attribution Guide*. 53 pp. RCI

Van Allen, Leroy. 2015. *Denticle & Die Impressions Morgan Dollar Attribution Guide*. 109 pp. RCI

Van Allen, Leroy. 2009. *1921 P Infrequently Reeded or Wide Reeding Morgan Dollar Attribution Guide*. 31 pp. RCI

Van Allen, Leroy. 2011 *Amazing Changing 1921 S VAM 1B Thorn Head Morgan Dollar*. 2011. 22 pp. RCI

Van Allen, Leroy. 2009. *1889 P Doubled Ear Morgan Dollar Attribution Guide*. 32 pp. RCI

Van Allen, Leroy. 2016. *Micro o and Other Counterfeit Morgan and Peace Dollars*. 191 pp RCI

Van Allen, Leroy. 2005. *Micro o Mint Mark on Morgan Dollars*. 32 pp. RCI

Van Allen, Leroy. 2005. *Die Markers for 1921 Morgan and Peace Proof Dollars*. 9 pp. RCI

Van Allen, Leroy and Baumgart, John. 1992-Date Various VAM Book Yearly Supplements. RCI

www.ingramcontent.com/pod-product-compliance
Ingram Content Group UK Ltd.
Pitfield, Milton Keynes, MK11 3LW, UK
UKHW062000290726
14090UKWH00021B/1302